# Re-enchanting The Unseen

*Angels, Demons, and Strange Beings From Time & Space*

Josh Robinson

Copyright © Josh Robinson

All rights reserved. No part of this book may be reproduced or used in any manner without the prior written permission of the copyright owner, except for the use of brief quotations in a book review.

To request permissions, contact the publisher at
pastorjoshrobinson@gmail.com

Cover art by Josh Robinson

## Dedication

This book is dedicated to all of my family and friends.

Thanks to my wife, Ally, and my daughter, Amelia, who have been patient with me taking time to write two books this year (2023). Without them, this book would not exist.

Thanks to The Sword and Staff and Shadow Appalachia crew, Ritchie, Ward, Travis, and Bo who have always encouraged me and sharpened me when it comes to conversations on the strange and weird. Without them, this book would not exist.

Also, thanks to all of the folks who read this book prior to its release and contributed to the conversation.

## Table of Contents

| | |
|---|---:|
| Introduction | 1 |
| 1. Angels & The Celestial Hierarchy | 6 |
| 2. The Powers of Darkness | 36 |
| 3. Demons | 55 |
| 4. UFO's & UAP | 75 |
| 5. Cryptids | 99 |
| 6. Ghosts | 129 |
| Appendix A | 145 |
| Appendix B | 163 |

# Introduction

This book is going to push you past your comfort zone. It's going to make you consider some things you've probably never considered before, or at the very least it's going to make you reconsider things you thought you already knew. That's by design. This book is meant to challenge you.

When we open the pages of the Bible, we find that we live in a world where the seen world and unseen world overlap and interact with one another. And make no mistake about it, the unseen world isn't just some abstract idea. It's an actual world with the kind of things you'd expect to find in the world. It's a world full of celestial flora and fauna, architecture, and inhabitants. Some of which you'll learn about here.

Why the need for a book that discusses such topics?

Because as a Christian and a pastor living in the 21st century, I see the effects of modernity all around us, even in the church. Rather than influencing the world, it appears to me that the world has influenced the church when it comes to the topic of the unseen realm. When most Christians think about the unseen world, they conjure an image in their minds of chubby babies with wings flying around God's throne and sitting on the clouds while playing harps for eternity. Many will be surprised that this book reveals that those who lived before our modern age had a very different vision of the unseen world; one that was teeming with life and enchanted.

This book is not meant to be a full treatment of this topic. It's really only the tip of the iceberg. But, my hope is that the Lord would use this particular book to help re-enchant the imagination of the church by recovering the cosmic imagery of the Bible and Christendom. I believe that if we can recover our traditional cosmic imagery, we will be able to make sense of much of the madness happening in our current world. Especially in regards to things life UFOS, UAP, sightings of strange, fantastical cryptids, and ghosts.

May the Lord use it for those purposes.

Josh Robinson, All Saints Hallows Eve 2023.

# Part One: Angels and Demons

# 1

# Angels & The Celestial Hierarchy

## Introduction

Let me start this question off by asking you a question. Do you have a category for angels?

Any Christian who has spent time reading the Bible will answer and say "of course!" However, one of the things that I have noted over the years as a pastor is that most people don't know what to do with angels beyond the idea of guardian angels. Many believe in the existence of angels, but that's about as far as it goes. When I ask "do you have a category for angels?" what I really mean isn't simply "do you believe in angels?" What I mean is when you look around in the world that you inhabit, do you believe that there are unseen celestial forces at work within it?

As modern people, we may have a difficult time believing that, but for the Christians who came before us, this wasn't even a debatable point.

Traditionally, the church has understood there to be three choirs or orders of angels. [1] These three choirs have different roles. One serves in close proximity to God, one serves in the governing of creation, and another serves in close proximity to humanity. In light of the Bible's three tier cosmology of highest heavens, lower heavens, and earth beneath, it would be accurate to think of each of the three choirs corresponding to these three realms.

The first choir serves in the highest heavens – which has traditionally been called the Empyrean. The second choir serves in the lower heavens which encompasses all of the cosmos to the heavenly skies of earth. The third choir serves in the earth and in the affairs of men. In light of the Bible's cosmology and realm distinction, I will use the terminology of Empyreal beings, Celestial beings, and Terrestrial beings.

## The First Choir of Angels

The first choir of angels can be thought of as those being closest in proximity to God. The three celestial beings who have

---

[1] It is generally assumed by scholars that the "angelic hierarchy" was an invention of the Medieval Church, particularly Pseudo-Dionysius the Areopagite. However, this is not the case as more access to ancient source material is available. It is clear that various understandings of angelic hierarchies existed going all the way back to the Second Temple Period and even in Early Church History in sources such as The Apostlic Constitution.

traditionally made up this choir are the Seraphim, Cherubim, and Ophanim (or sometimes called Thrones). [2] These celestial beings are who I am referring to as the Empyreal beings because they serve in the highest heaven – in the Empyrean.

## Seraphim

Among the celestial entities mentioned in the Holy Scriptures, the Seraphim stand out with distinct features and roles that emphasize their proximity and service to Yahweh. Their name itself suggests a fiery or burning nature, further strengthening their ethereal significance.

A primary reference to the Seraphim can be found in the Book of Isaiah. There, they are described as fiery, flying serpents possessing six wings. Specifically, in Isaiah 6:2, the prophet recounts a vision where he saw the Lord seated on a throne, high and exalted, with the train of His robe filling the temple. Above Him were Seraphim, each with six wings: "With two wings they covered their faces, with two they covered their feet, and with two they were flying." This imagery not only conveys their humility and

---

[2] Many Christians will be familiar with the Thrones but likely not the Ophanim. Ophanim is the ancient Hebrew word for "wheels" on the throne of God in Ezekiel 1:15-21, 10:9-13. One of the Dead Sea Scrolls (4Q405) identifies them as angels, and 1 Enoch 61:10, 71:7 portrays them as a class of celestial beings who along with the Seraphim and Cherubim who never sleep, but guard the sacred space of God's throne in the highest heaven. Thrones and Ophanim are synonymous.

reverence before God, as they shielded themselves from His radiance, but also emphasizes their ceaseless loyalty and service to the Divine.

Their primary role seems to be intertwined with the eternal contemplation and glorification of God. Isaiah 6:3 recounts their heavenly hymns: "And they were calling to one another: 'Holy, holy, holy is the Lord Almighty; the whole earth is full of His glory.'" Their voices were so powerful that they shook the very foundations of the thresholds. Through their praises, the Seraphim exemplify a constant and fervent devotion to Yahweh, reminding all of creation of the unparalleled holiness of the Almighty, serving as a powerful testament to the magnificence, sanctity, and majesty of the Creator they ceaselessly adore.

## Cherubim

The second celestial being in the first choir is the Cherubim. The Cherubim are particularly intriguing due to their multifaceted appearance and sacred duties.

A description of the Cherubim can be found in the Book of Ezekiel. In a profound vision, the prophet Ezekiel depicts them as tetramorphic beings, bearing a unique combination of four distinct forms: that of men, lions, oxen, and eagles (Ez. 1:5-14). They are also described as ablaze, with a fiery intensity that further accentuates their divine nature.

The Cherubim are consistently associated with the protection and guardianship of sacred spaces. A prime example of this protective role can be seen in the Book of Genesis. After the Fall, when Adam and Eve were banished from the Garden of Eden, God placed the Cherubim at the eastern entrance of the garden, along with a flaming sword that turned every way, to guard the way to the tree of life (Gen. 3:24). Their presence, paired with the flaming sword, highlights their purpose as stalwart guardians against any unwarranted access of anything profane into paradise.

Furthermore, their sacred guardianship extends beyond Eden. The Holy of Holies, the innermost sanctum of the Tabernacle and later the Temple, where the Ark of the Covenant resided, was also under their watchful eyes. In fact, representations of Cherubim were embroidered into the veil that separated the Holy of Holies from the rest of the Tabernacle (Ex. 26:31) and were crafted atop the Ark of the Covenant itself, their wings outspread in protective posture (Ex. 25:18-20).

In other biblical narratives, the Cherubim are also depicted as surrounding or even upholding the very throne of God, reinforcing the notion of their proximity to the Divine and their integral role in the heavenly hierarchy.

In sum, the Cherubim, with their unique tetramorphic appearance and their consistent association with guarding the most sacred, exemplify the profound reverence and protective fervor that the Divine commands. Through them, the sanctity of God's spaces—be it Eden, the Holy of Holies, or His throne room—is fervently preserved and shielded from any profanity.

**Ophanim**

The third celestial being in the first choir is the Ophanim, often referred to as "Thrones," possess a distinct role in the angelic hierarchy and a strikingly unparalleled appearance.

Derived from the prophet Ezekiel's visions, the Ophanim are intricately described with great detail. They appear as wheels, with a likeness to beryl, a precious stone known for its clear and shining appearance. But these aren't just ordinary wheels; they are wheels within wheels, evoking an image of complex interlocking mechanics. Adding to their awe-inducing appearance, their rims are described as being "full of eyes all around" (Ez. 1:16-21). This multitude of eyes symbolizes their unwavering vigilance and all-encompassing awareness, embodying the omniscience of the God they serve.

Yet, the Ophanim aren't merely static, decorative entities. They are imbued with a profound purpose. As described in Ezekiel's account, these wheels are filled with the "Spirit of the Living God," which not only grants them life and movement but also connects them deeply to the divine essence of God. Their primary function is to serve as the wheels of God's throne chariot, making them an integral part of the heavenly vehicle that facilitates God's movement.

The divine chariot's movement is synchronized with that of the Cherubim, as described in Ezekiel 1:21, "When the living creatures moved, the wheels beside them moved; and when the living creatures rose from the ground, the wheels also rose." This intricate dance between the Ophanim and the Cherubim showcases a harmonious union in serving the will of God.
In essence, the Ophanim, with their intricate design and divine purpose, underscore the majesty and grandeur of God's presence. Acting as the very wheels on which the throne chariot

of the Almighty moves, they not only symbolize the omnipresence of God but also emphasize His ability to oversee and interact with all of creation. Through them, we are reminded of the vastness of the divine machinery and the intricate details that uphold the sanctity of God's dominion.

## The Second Choir of Angels

The second choir of angels can be thought of as being lower in the hierarchy than the first choir. Not necessarily because they aren't as important, are lower in rank, or aren't as powerful, but rather because they have different God ordained roles.

From what we gather in Scripture about this choir of angels, this particular order seems to be at work not in the highest heavens like the first choir, but in the celestial realm of the cosmos, which means they are not as close in proximity to God as the first choir. This is why the church has traditionally put them lower in the hierarchy than the first choir. This order of angels that most work in the nature of the cosmos are the Dominions, Virtues, and Powers. These are the beings that I refer to as the Celestial beings.

## Dominions

When we look at Scripture, the Dominions are grouped together with other known angelic beings. In Colossians 1:16-17, the Apostle Paul stating the preeminence of Christ says:

> "because all things in the heavens and on the earth were created by him, things visible and things invisible, whether thrones or dominions or rulers or powers, all things were created through him and for him, 17 and he himself is before all things, and in him all things are held together. . ." - Colossians 1:16-17 LEB

We also see Dominions mentioned in Ephesians 1:21 as well. There, the Apostle Paul writes that God raised His Son, Jesus the anointed one from the dead and seated him at His right hand in the heavenly places "far above all rule and authority and power and dominion and every name that is named." Paul writes in Ephesians 1:15-23:

> "Because of this I also, hearing of ⌊your faith⌋ in the Lord Jesus and your love for all the saints, 16 do not cease giving thanks for you, making mention in my prayers, 17 that the God of our Lord Jesus Christ, ⌊the glorious Father⌋,* may

give you a spirit of wisdom* and revelation in the knowledge of him 18 (the eyes of your hearts having been enlightened), so that you may know what is the hope of his calling, what are the riches of the glory of his inheritance among the saints, 19 and what is the surpassing greatness of his power toward us who believe, according to the working of his mighty strength 20 which he has worked in Christ, raising him from the dead and seating him at his right hand in the heavenly places, 21 above all principality and authority and power and dominion and every name named, not only in this age but also in the coming one, 22 and he subjected all things under his feet and gave him as head over all things to the church, 23 which is his body, the fullness of the one who fills all things in every way." - Ephesians 1:15-23

Commenting on this, New Testament scholar P. W. van der Horst states:

"In Eph 1:21 κυριότης is part of an enumeration of supernatural powers. The author says that God has raised →Jesus →Christ from the dead and seated him at his right hand in the heavenly places "far above all rule and authority and power and dominion and every name that is named" (ὑπεράνω πάσης ἀρχῆς καὶ ἐξουσίας καὶ δυνάμεως καὶ

> κυριότητος καὶ παντὸς ὀνόματος ὀνομαζομένου, Principalities [→Archai], →Authorities, Power [→Dynamis], →Name). Col 1:16 states that in Jesus Christ "all things in heaven and on earth were created, things visible and invisible, whether thrones or dominions or rulers or powers" (εἴτε θρόνοι εἴτε κυριότητες εἴτε ἀρχαὶ εἴτε ἐξουσίαι). In both instances the conviction is clearly stated that all angelic (and demonic) powers are completely subordinated to Christ; being his own creatures, they are his servants and hence no longer a threat to be feared by God's children."[3]

It's clear that both Ephesians and Colossians have spiritual powers in mind and not just earthly powers. The point that the Apostle Paul is making is that all angelic (and demonic) powers are subordinated to Christ because He is their creator and because He has been enthroned at the right hand of God through His resurrection from the dead and His ascension to the right hand of God the Father.

Other than these two explicit mentions of Dominions, information about this class of celestial being is sparse in the Bible. However, the *International Standard Bible Encyclopedia,* another scholarly

---

[3] P. W. van der Horst, "Dominion," ed. Karel van der Toorn and Bob Becking, *Dictionary of Deities and Demons in the Bible* (Leiden; Boston; Köln; Grand Rapids, MI; Cambridge: Brill; Eerdmans, 1999), 262.

source, suggests that Jude 1:8 and 2 Peter 2:10 probably should be interpreted as angels as well, but it's difficult to know. [4]

So, the question we must ask now is why is the information in the Bible sparse? And, where are the inspired writers of Scripture getting their angelology from if Scripture doesn't make reference to them much, especially the Hebrew Bible?

Information is sparse because it was assumed in the ancient world. In other words, when something is common knowledge, we typically don't spend much time citing sources or trying to explain it. We just assume it's valid. This is likely what's occurring with Dominions in the Bible. The idea that these particular spiritual beings were beings at work in the heavenly places was just assumed and there was no reason to explain it because it was common knowledge to Jewish people in the Second Temple Period.

---

[4] See entry from The International Standard Bible Encyclopedia.

"DOMINION, dŏ-min'yun: In Eph 1:21; Col 1:16 the word so tr (κυριότης, kuriótēs) appears to denote a rank or order of angels. The same word is probably to be so interpreted in Jude ver 8 (AV and RV "dominion"), and in 2 Pet 2:10 (AV "government," RV "dominion")."

James Orr et al., eds., "Dominion," *The International Standard Bible Encyclopaedia* (Chicago: The Howard-Severance Company, 1915), 869.

But, where did they get this belief? If Biblical references are sparse, what were they basing their knowledge on? To the surprise of many, we learn that they were basing it off of Second Temple source material such as 1 and 2 Enoch.

In 2 Enoch 20:1, the pseudepigraphal writes:

> "And those men lifted me up from there, and they carried me up to the 7$^{th}$ heaven. And I saw there an exceptionally great light, and all the fiery armies of the great archangels, and the incorporeal forces and the dominions and the origins and the authorities, the cherubim and the seraphim and the many-eyed thrones; and regiments and the shining otanim stations. And I was terrified, and I trembled with a great fear."

The thought in the Second Temple Period and even into early church history is that these particular spiritual beings had been tasked with governance of the cosmos under the rule of Yahweh. As we noted already, Dominions is κυριότης in Greek which means "lord" which denotes the power to rule.

Commenting on this during the Middle Ages, Thomas Aquinas in his Summa Theologiae:

> "It belongs to the first hierarchy to consider the end; to the middle one belongs the universal disposition of what is to be done; and to the last belongs the application of this disposition to the effect, which is the carrying out of the work; for it is clear that these three things exist in every kind of operation." [5]

To sum up Aquinas, it is the second choir of angels that carries out "what is to be done" in creation. The responsibility of the Dominions in this particular order is "lordship" or "to rule" over this particular choir as a kind of head of the lower choirs who is also under the lordship of Yahweh as the "lord of lords."

**Powers**

The second celestial being in this choir of angels is the Powers or δύναμις in Greek. Traditionally, these spiritual beings have been referred to as Virtues. This is because Jerome translated δύναμις as Virtutem in translation of the Greek New Testament into Latin. For our purposes, I prefer the term Powers because it best gets at their role in creation. They are the powers at work in the cosmos, including the earth.

---

[5] Thomas Aquians, "Question 108, Article 6: The Angelic Degrees of Hierarchies and Orders," *Summa Theologiae*, https://www.newadvent.org/summa/1108.htm.

Paul makes reference to them in Ephesians 1:21, which is a passage we've already looked at. There he says that Christ has risen from the dead and seated at the right hand of the Father in the heavenly places, above all rule, authority, and power, and lordship, and every name named not only in this age, but also in the age to come.

Another New Testament scholar, H. D. Betz, notes that the term Powers has a broad lexical use. It informs us that:

> "In most biblical instances, however, 'power' is regarded as an attribute either of God who is in control of all powers, or of subservient divine agents acting on his behalf through delegated powers. In the biblical and post-biblical literature these powers include →angels, →demons, →stars, →Stoicheia, and the →Holy Spirit; in the NT, in addition, →Christ is integrated in the hierarchy." [6]

The interesting thing to note here is that Powers include not just angels, demons, and stars, but also stoicheia. This Greek term

---

[6] H. D. Betz, "Dynamis," ed. Karel van der Toorn, Bob Becking, and Pieter W. van der Horst, *Dictionary of Deities and Demons in the Bible* (Leiden; Boston; Köln; Grand Rapids, MI; Cambridge: Brill; Eerdmans, 1999), 268.

may be unfamiliar to readers, but this Greek word is translated in most English Bible translations as "elemental spirits" (LEB) or "elementary principles (ESV) or "elemental things" (NASB) or "elements" (KJV, NKJV). The translation of stoicheia as "elementary principles" and "elemental things" and "elements" is an unfortunate translation because it removes the supernatural backdrop. When Paul uses this term in Galatians 4:3-9 and Colossians 2:8-20, he is using it in reference to spiritual beings that are powers over the elements of creation.

In other words, the inspired writers of Scripture, in their context of the ancient world, understood Elemental Spirits to be the powers at work in the elements of creation like water, earth, fire, wind, and the rest of the cosmos.

*The Lexham Bible Dictionary* affirms this understanding of Elemental Spirits, stating:

> In Colossians 2:8, 20, where Paul uses stoicheia in a discussion of Christ's lordship over the cosmic powers and the Colossians' worship of angels (2:18), the term likely refers to "elemental spirits" (ESV, NRSV) or "elemental spiritual forces" (NIV), rather than "elementary principles"

(NASB95), "basic principles" (NKJV), or "rudiments" (KJV). . . In Galatians 4:3, 9, "elementary principles" (ESV), "elemental things" (NASB95), or simply "elements" (KJV, NKJV), all seem to fit. However, the idea of enslavement in Gal 4:3, elaborated in Gal 4:8 with reference to false gods, also supports a translation of "elemental spirits" (NRSV), or "elemental spiritual forces" (NIV), especially in light of the possible influence of Jewish apocalyptic writings (Lee, "Interpreting," 56–58) and the prevalent belief that nature was controlled by spirit beings (Hincks, "Meaning," 190–92). As Lee states, "To live under the law means to be subservient to the elemental spirits of the universe." [7]

This line of thought is also present in some of the literature of the Second Temple Period. 1 Enoch 61:10 reads:

> "And He will summon all the host of the heavens, and all the holy ones above, and the host of God, the Cherubic, Seraphin and Ophannin, and all the angels of power, and all the angels of principalities, and the Elect One, and the other powers on the earth (and) over the water."

---

[7] Michael R. Jones, "Elemental Spirit," ed. John D. Barry et al., *The Lexham Bible Dictionary* (Bellingham, WA: Lexham Press, 2016).

Notice that there are "powers on the earth and over the water." These are the elemental spirits, also known as the Virtues or Powers. It was also thought during medieval times that since these were the spiritual beings over the elements and nature of those cosmos, they were the ones whom Yahweh used as means to the end of working the miraculous.

## Authorities

The third and last celestial being in the second choir is the Authorities. Traditionally, the church has called these Powers as well. Jerome translated ἐξουσία as potestatem in the Latin Vulgate, however, to avoid confusion with the last class of celestial beings, and because ἐξουσία and corresponds to the verb ἔξεστιν which means "have permission, possibility, authority," it's best to refer to them as the Authorities. [8]

The role of these spiritual beings is exactly what their names imply. They are the ones who have permission from Yahweh to have authority. But, authority over what?

---

[8] H. D. Betz, "Authorities," ed. Karel van der Toorn, Bob Becking, and Pieter W. van der Horst, *Dictionary of Deities and Demons in the Bible* (Leiden; Boston; Köln; Grand Rapids, MI; Cambridge: Brill; Eerdmans, 1999), 124.

Traditionally, it was understood that they were the ones who had authority over evil spirits. They can be seen as a kind of warrior class of spiritual being. Thomas Aquinas in his *Summa Theologiae* said:

> "Dionysius (Coel. Hier. vii) explains the names of the orders accordingly as they befit the spiritual perfections they signify. Gregory, on the other hand, in expounding these names (Hom. xxxiv in Evang.) seems to regard more the exterior ministrations; for he says that "angels are so called as announcing the least things; and the archangels in the greatest; by the virtues miracles are wrought; by the powers (Authorities) hostile powers are repulsed." [9]

Again, like the Dominions, there are no antecedents for the New Testaments usage of ἐξουσία (exousiai). The inspired writers of the New Testament seem to have received a tradition that existed in their day that the Authorities were a class of angelic beings that existed and were at work in the cosmos though it's not found in the Bible prior to the writing of the New Testament. This didn't mean that they considered these traditions found in Jewish literature to be on par with the canon of Scripture, but it does

---

[9] Thomas Aquians, "Question 108, Article 5: The Angelic Degrees of Hierarchies and Orders," *Summa Theologiae*, https://www.newadvent.org/summa/1108.htm.

mean that they considered there to be some truths contained within them.

Commenting on this, Betz states:

> "There are no antecedents for the NT usage of exousiai in the LXX or other pre-Christian Hellenistic texts. However, its origin must be sought in apocalyptic (see 1 Enoch 61:10; 2 Enoch 20:1 (J); Ass. Isa. 1:4; T. Levi 3:8; cf. 1 Enoch 9:5 (Gk); T. Levi 18:12; Apoc. Bar. (Gk) 12:3; T. Abr. 9:8; 13:11; T. Sol. 1:1; 15:11; 18:3; 22:15, 20; titulus B I [p *98 ed. McCown]), in magic (see PGM I.215–216; IV.1193–1194; XII.147; XVII.a.5), and perhaps in Gnosticism (see Corp. Herm. I.13, 14, 15, 28, 32; XVI.14; Frg. XXIII [Korē Kosmou] 55, 58, 63). Thus, the linguistic evidence is ambiguous with regard to any specific origin of the usage. Precise Hebrew or Aramaic equivalents or antecedents are missing (cf. Str-B 3.581–3.584; Michl 1965:9–80); in Latin translations the word potestas is used." [10]

---

[10] H. D. Betz, "Authorities," ed. Karel van der Toorn, Bob Becking, and Pieter W. van der Horst, *Dictionary of Deities and Demons in the Bible* (Leiden; Boston; Köln; Grand Rapids, MI; Cambridge: Brill; Eerdmans, 1999), 124.

## The Third Choir of Angels

The third choir of angels can be thought of as being the lowest of the choirs. Again, as we saw with the second choir, this isn't necessarily because they aren't as important, are lower in rank, or aren't as powerful, but rather because they have different God ordained roles.

From what we gather in Scripture about this choir of angels, this particular order seems to be at work not in the highest heavens or in the middle heavens like the first and second choirs, but in the earth where humans reside, which means they are not as close in proximity to God as the first choir or even the second choir. This order of angels that most work in the realm of the earth are the Principalities, Archangels, and Angels. These are the beings that I refer to as the Terrestrial beings, and unlike the angels in the second choir, the Bible has much to say about these spiritual beings.

### Principalities

The first spiritual being in this choir of angels is the Principalities or the Ἀρχαί (archē). It also is used in a more concrete sense referring to those who rule or govern, i.e. 'magistrate', 'ruler', 'governor' (Luke 12:11). When used with the latter meaning, archē belongs to the same semantic subdomain as archōn. [11]

When we look at Scripture, we see that these spiritual beings are closely related to the rulership of geographical areas. This idea of rulership of geographical areas is closely tied to the idea of territorial spirits.

One of the places where we see this spelled out explicitly is in Daniel 10:18-21. There, the prophet Daniel has an encounter with the Archangel Michael, who is the "prince" of Israel. We learn that he was apparently delayed in coming to speak to Daniel because he was fighting against the Prince of Persia, which is an obvious supernatural entity in this context, since the Archangel Michael is also identified as the Prince of Israel. Daniel writes:

> "18 And ⌊he again touched⌋ me, ⌊the one in the form of a human⌋, and he strengthened me. 19 And he said, "You must not fear, O beloved man. ⌊Peace be to you⌋; be strong and be courageous!" And ⌊when he spoke⌋ with me, I was strengthened and I said, "Let my lord speak, for you have

---

[11] D. E. Aune, "Archai," ed. Karel van der Toorn, Bob Becking, and Pieter W. van der Horst, *Dictionary of Deities and Demons in the Bible* (Leiden; Boston; Köln; Grand Rapids, MI; Cambridge: Brill; Eerdmans, 1999), 77.

strengthened me." 20 Then he asked, "Do you know why I have come to you? And now I return to fight against the prince of Persia and I myself am going, and look, the prince of Javan will come. 21 However, I will tell you ⌊what is inscribed⌋ in the book of truth, and there is not one who contends with me against these beings ⌊except⌋ Michael, your prince." - Daniel 10:18-21 LEB

Here, we learn that there were particular angelic beings in charge of nations, particularly Persia, Greece (Javan) and even Israel. The term "prince" is related to "principality." A "principality" is a nation-state ruled over by a prince. In our modern context, you can think of it as being similar to a "municipality" that is ruled over by "municipal offices."

This is also present in the Second Temple Period as well, especially in the Enochian literature. Again, 1 Enoch 61:10 reads:

> "And He will summon all the host of the heavens, and all the holy ones above, and the host of God, the Cherubic, Seraphin and Ophannin, and all the angels of power, and all the angels of principalities, and the Elect One, and the other powers on the earth (and) over the water."

It's also used in the account of the flood in 1 Enoch 6:1-8 of the fallen angels that lusted after the daughters of men. The fallen angels that were involved in the creation of the giants are called "chiefs."

> "And it came to pass when the children of men had multiplied that in those days were born unto them beautiful and comely daughters. 2 And the angels, the children of the heaven, saw and lusted after them, and said to one another: 'Come, let us choose us wives from among the children of men and beget us children.' 3 And Semjâzâ, who was their leader, said unto them: 'I fear ye will not indeed agree to do this deed, and I alone shall have to pay the penalty of a great sin.' 4 And they all answered him and said: 'Let us all swear an oath, and all bind ourselves by mutual imprecations not to abandon this plan but to do this thing.' 5 Then sware they all together and bound themselves by mutual imprecations upon it. 6 And they were in all two hundred; who descended ⌈in the days⌉ of Jared on the summit of Mount Hermon, and they called it Mount Hermon, because they had sworn and bound themselves by mutual imprecations upon it. 7 And these are the names of their

leaders: Sêmîazâz, their leader, Arâkîba, Râmêêl, Kôkabîêl, Tâmîêl, Râmîêl, Dânêl, Êzêqêêl, Barâqîjâl, Asâêl, Armârôs, Batârêl, Anânêl, Zaqîêl, Samsâpêêl, Satarêl, Tûrêl, Jômjâêl, Sariêl. 8 These are their chiefs of tens."

Commenting on this, American New Testament scholar D.E. Aune states:

"In 1 Enoch 6:8 (preserved in Gk and Aram in addition to Eth), archai is used of twenty named angels or →Watchers, each of whom commands ten angels of lesser status. This angelic organization appears to have a military origin, for the Israelite army was arranged under leaders of thousands, hundreds, fifties and tens (Exod 18:21, 25; Deut 1:15; 1 Macc 3:55; 1QM 3.16–17; 4.1–5, 15–17). Josephus refers to the organization of the Maccabean army in 1 Macc 3:55 as "the old traditional manner" (Ant. 12.301). In the LXX Exod 18:21, 25 and 1 Macc 3:55 the term dekadarchai is used for commanders of the lowest level of military organization, which was also common in the Hellenistic world (Xenophon Cyr. 8.1.14; Polybius 6.25.2; Josephus War 2.578; Arrian Anab. 7.23.3)." [12]

---

[12] D. E. Aune, "Archai," ed. Karel van der Toorn, Bob Becking, and Pieter W. van der Horst, *Dictionary of Deities and Demons in the Bible* (Leiden; Boston; Köln; Grand Rapids, MI; Cambridge: Brill; Eerdmans, 1999), 78.

## Archangels

The second spiritual being in this choir of angels is the Archangel or ἀρχάγγελος (archangelos).

There are two Archangels mentioned in the Bible. Those are the Archangel's Michael and Gabriel. Most are familiar with the Archangel Michael, but Gabriel is one people are less familiar with. He also makes an appearance in the Book of Daniel (Dan. 8:16, 9:21).

When we look at Scripture, it appears that these angels have been tasked with keeping watch over God's people and to act as "princes" for God's people and over other angels, as seen in Daniel 10.

Thomas Aquinas notes this in his *Summa Theologiae*, stating:

> "The "Archangels," according to Dionysius (Coel. Hier. ix), are between the "Principalities" and the "Angels." A medium compared to one extreme seems like the other, as participating in the nature of both extremes; thus tepid seems cold compared to hot, and hot compared to cold. So the "Archangels" are called the "angel princes"; forasmuch

as they are princes as regards the "Angels," and angels as regards the Principalities. But according to Gregory (Hom. xxiv in Ev.) they are called "Archangels," because they preside over the one order of the "Angels"; as it were, announcing greater things." [13]

In literature from the Second Temple Period, there are more Archangels named. The names listed are typically Michael, Gabriel, Raphael, and Uriel in most manuscripts of 1 Enoch 9, 10, 40:9; 54:6; 71:8–9, 13; 1QM 9, 15; Apoc. Mos. 40; seven 1 Enoch 20).

**Angels**

The third and last spiritual being in the third choir is angels or מלאך (malak) in Hebrew.

All throughout Scripture, we see that the role of angels is exactly what their name implies. They are "messengers" who proclaim news from heaven to humanity.

---

[13] Thomas Aquians, "Question 108, Article 5: The Angelic Degrees of Hierarchies and Orders," *Summa Theologiae*, https://www.newadvent.org/summa/1108.htm.

Of course, the most well-known example of this is the angel Gabriel, who appears to be an Archangel, who announced to Mary that she would conceive the Lord.

> "Now in the sixth month, the angel Gabriel was sent from God to a town of Galilee ⌊named⌋ Nazareth, 27 to a virgin legally promised in marriage to a man ⌊named⌋ Joseph of the house of David. And the name of the virgin was Mary. 28 And he came to her and* said, "Greetings, favored one! The Lord is with you." 29 But she was greatly perplexed at the statement, and was pondering what sort of greeting this might be. 30 And the angel said to her, "Do not be afraid, Mary, for you have found favor with God. 31 And behold, you will conceive in the womb and will give birth to a son, and you will call his name Jesus. 32 This one will be great, and he will be called the Son of the Most High, and the Lord God will give him the throne of his father David. 33 And he will reign over the house of Jacob ⌊forever⌋, and of his kingdom there will be no end. 34 And Mary said to the angel, "How will this be, since I have not had sexual relations with a man?" 35 And the angel answered and* said to her, "The Holy Spirit will come upon you, and the power of the Most

High will overshadow you. Therefore also the one to be born will be called holy, the Son of God." - Luke 1:26-35 LEB

Thomas Aquinas sums up the

"Angel means "messenger." So all the heavenly spirits, so far as they make known Divine things, are called "angels." But the superior angels enjoy a certain excellence, as regards this manifestation, from which the superior orders are denominated. The lowest order of angels possess no excellence above the common manifestation; and therefore it is denominated from manifestation only; and thus the common name remains as it were proper to the lowest order, as Dionysius says (Coel. Hier. v). Or we may say that the lowest order can be specially called the order of "angels," forasmuch as they announce things to us immediately." [14]

## Conclusion

So, why does having this category for angels matter?

---

[14] Thomas Aquians, "Question 108, Article 5: The Angelic Degrees of Hierarchies and Orders," *Summa Theologiae*, https://www.newadvent.org/summa/1108.htm.

To put it simply, it changes the way you view everything. Most modern Christians do not have a category for angels. However, when we look at the ancient world, it's clear that they had a vision of the cosmos that was filled with spiritual beings. This is true even of the inspired writers of Scripture.

This can also change the way that you view natural phenomena and world events, because you realize that even though you cannot see it, there is an unseen hand behind all of it. When natural disasters occur, when nations war against other nations, when things happen in the heavenlies, the biblical writers would have thought there was something going on there in the unseen.

# 2

# The Powers of Darkness

## Introduction

When we delve into the pages of the Bible, a rich tapestry of spiritual beings within the heavenly host unfolds, revealing a similar diversity within the realm of darkness. The biblical exploration of the unseen realm uncovers not just demons, but also ancient and more insidious adversaries that wield their influence over the world and its affairs. Surprisingly, demons emerge as latecomers to this cosmic drama, occupying a lower rung in the infernal hierarchy.

In the previous chapter, we examined the Bible's teachings concerning the angelic hierarchy. As we delve further into the scriptures, a pattern emerges: fallen spiritual beings from every level of the angelic hierarchy constitute a shadowy and malevolent order.

# The First Choir

### Seraphim

While the Bible does not explicitly mention fallen Seraphim, an intriguing perspective can be gleaned by exploring the iconography of the Ancient Near East. This perspective suggests that various cultures within the region revered winged serpent beings.

Intriguingly, the iconography of these ancient cultures often depicted winged serpent figures, hinting at the potential existence of beings at least akin to the biblical Seraphim. Although the Bible does not explicitly label these figures as fallen Seraphim, the presence of such iconography raises thought-provoking possibilities.

The worship of these winged serpent beings by different peoples in the Ancient Near East adds a layer of complexity to the understanding of spiritual entities. While not definitive evidence of fallen Seraphim, this iconographic exploration underscores the rich tapestry of beliefs and cosmologies present in the ancient world.

Commenting on this, Hebrew Bible professor T. N. D. Mettinger states:

> "The study of the ancient Near Eastern evidence, esp. iconographic representations, has been instrumental in the attempts to clarify the meaning and background of the seraphim. While some scholars have hinted that the seven thunders of →Baal and his lightning bolts or their iconography might provide illuminating parallels (cf. ANEP no. 655), there is now an emerging consensus that the Egyptian uraeus serpent is the original source of the seraphim motif (Joines 1974; De Savignac 1972). This interpretation was worked out by Keel (1977:70–124) who was able to adduce iconographic evidence showing that the uraeus motif was well known in Palestine from the Hyksos period through the end of the Iron Age (on scarabs and seals). During the 8th century bce the two-winged and, in Judah especially the four-winged, uraeus is a well attested motif on seals, while six-winged uraei do not seem to occur. Friezes with uraei (without wings) are found in Egyptian and Phoenician chapels. The English term "uraeus" is a loan-word from Greek which was in turn taken from the Egyptian word for the cobra figure worn on the forehead of Egyptian gods and kings, whom the cobra protects by

means of her "fire" (poison). Among the Egyptian designations for the uraeus one finds the word ꜣḫt, "flame"."[15]

In summary, Mettinger suggests that the Israelite concept of Seraphim has its origins in ancient Egyptian symbolism, particularly the "Uraeus." This term "Uraeus," borrowed from Greek, originates from the Egyptian word "Wadjet," associated with a serpent goddess. Wadjet was revered as the guardian of Lower Egypt, using her protective "fire," which likely contributes to the imagery of the "flaming serpent" found in the Bible.

Mike Heiser, another Hebrew Bible scholar, also makes note of this, stating:

> "It is common for interpreters to presume the lemma behind seraphim is the verb śārap, which means "to burn." As recent research has shown, this is only part of the picture. As I noted in The Unseen Realm, "It is more likely that seraphim derives from the Hebrew noun śārap ("serpent"), which in turn is drawn from Egyptian throne guardian terminology and conceptions. As recent research

---

[15] T. N. D. Mettinger, "Seraphim," ed. Karel van der Toorn, Bob Becking, and Pieter W. van der Horst, *Dictionary of Deities and Demons in the Bible* (Leiden; Boston; Köln; Grand Rapids, MI; Cambridge: Brill; Eerdmans, 1999), 743.

demonstrates, the Egyptian Uraeus serpent, drawn from two species of Egyptian cobras, fits all the elements of the supernatural seraphim who attend Yahweh's holy presence in Isaiah 6. The relevant cobra species spit "burning" venom, can expand wind flanges of skin on either side of their bodies — considered "wings" in antiquity — when threatened, and are (obviously) serpentine. As Joines notes, the protective nature of the uraeus cobra is evident: "A function of the uraeus is to protect the pharaoh and sacred objects by breathing out fire on his enemies." [16]

It is reasonable to assert that within the worldview of the scriptural authors, the existence of seraphim encompassed both those who remained loyal to Yahweh and those who rebelled against Him, also serving as deities for pagan nations.

### Cherubim

Genesis 3 introduces us to the original rebel in the Garden of Eden. This narrative portrays Satan, once counted among God's council servants, rebelling against Him and leading humanity into disobedience.

---

[16] Michael S. Heiser, *Angels: What The Bible Really Says About The Heavenly Host* (Bellingham, WA; Lexham Press, 2018), 26-27.

Moving forward to Ezekiel 28, the prophet delivers a prophecy concerning the King of Tyre. The word of the Lord reaches Ezekiel, instructing him to convey this prophecy to the king who, in his arrogance, proclaims himself as divine and exalts his position to that of gods. As Ezekiel receives the divine message, a noteworthy detail emerges. He writes:

> 14 You were an anointed guardian cherub,
> and I placed you on ⌊God's holy mountain⌋;
> you walked in the midst of stones of fire.
> 15 You were blameless in your ways
> from the day ⌊when you were created⌋,
> until wickedness was found in you.
> 16 In the abundance of your trading,
> they filled the midst of you with violence, and you sinned;
> and I cast you as a profane thing from the mountain of God,
> and I expelled you, the guardian cherub,
> from the midst of the stones of fire.
> 17 Your heart was proud because of your beauty;
> you ruined your wisdom because of your splendor.
> I threw you on the ground ⌊before⌋ kings;
> I have exposed you ⌊for viewing⌋."

In this context, Ezekiel draws a parallel between the King of Tyre and the fallen guardian cherub who once resided in the garden amidst the fiery stones but was subsequently cast down to be publicly revealed before the eyes of worldly kings. Similar to the King of Tyre, this guardian cherub arrogantly declared, "I am a god, I sit in the seat of gods." His vanity was fueled by his own beauty. The unmistakable implication is that the guardian cherub referred to by Ezekiel is none other than Satan, the original archetypal adversary of God.

Commenting on this, Heiser notes:

> "One of God's heavenly-council servants presents himself to Eve as a serpent with the intent to deceive. Many incorrectly presume, however, that the language of Genesis 3 can be parsed only as a talking snake. There are other options, particularly after the full text of the Hebrew Bible existed. Other passages contribute elements to the story. For example, the divine being of Eden is referred to as a cherub (kērûb) in Ezekiel 28:14) — specifically a "guardian (hassôkēk) cherub." [17]

---

[17] Michael S. Heiser, *Demons: What The Bible Really Says About The Powers of Darkness* (Bellingham, WV; Lexham Press, 2020), 65.

When examining the cherubim in a state of righteousness before God, we observe their role in safeguarding sacred spaces, upholding the divine throne, and offering majestic praises. Conversely, we can envision fallen cherubim engaging in the opposite. They inhabit defiled areas, war against God and His heavenly host, and curse Him and His goodness.

**Ophanim**

As we progress through the biblical narrative, we also encounter references to fallen ophanim or thrones. The exact timing of their fall is not explicitly mentioned in the Bible, but it is evident that they are included among the entities over whom Christ has achieved victory.

Paul in Colossians 1:13-17 writes:

> "He has rescued us from the domain of darkness and transferred us* to the kingdom of the Son ⌐he loves⌐, 14 in whom we have the redemption, the forgiveness of sins, 15 who is the image of the invisible God, the firstborn over all* creation, 16 because all things in the heavens and on the earth were created by him, things visible and things invisible, whether thrones or dominions or rulers or powers, all things

were created through him and for him, 17 and he himself is before all things, and in him all things are held together."

At the heart of Paul's theology of the cross is the concept that through His death and resurrection, Jesus Christ has accomplished atonement for the sins of humanity, purifying them from their impurities. However, it's crucial to observe that within the same passage, there exists another equally central element in Paul's theology of the cross—a cosmic dimension that cannot be overlooked.

This cosmic element revolves around the notion that Jesus Christ has not only provided redemption from the dominion of darkness through His work but has also effectuated a profound transformation in the fabric of the cosmos. The resurrection of Jesus Christ from the dead stands as a testament to His vindication as the preeminent figure among all of creation, embodying the very image of the unseen God. As a consequence, He now holds supreme authority and power over all aspects of existence—be it in the celestial realms or upon the earthly plane. Every realm, whether it be thrones, dominions, rulers, or powers, owes its existence to Him, as all were brought into being by His creative mastery.

It is for this reason that the early church fathers such as Saint Athanasius declared with authority:

> "When the sun has come, darkness prevails no longer; any of it that may be left anywhere is driven away. So also, now that the Divine epiphany of the Word of God has taken place, the darkness of idols prevails no more, and all parts of the world in every direction are enlightened by His teaching." [18]

## The Second Choir

### Dominions, Powers, and Authorities

The Bible provides evidence of fallen counterparts among the spiritual beings in the second choir of angels as well. In Ephesians 1:20-23, Paul again echoes this thought that we also saw in Colossians. He writes:

> "He has worked in Christ, raising* him from the dead and seating him* at his right hand in the heavenly places, 21 above all principalities and authority and power and domination and every name named, not only in this age but

---

[18] Saint Athanasius, *On The Incarnation* (Yonkers, NY; St. Vladimir's Seminary Press), 79-80.

> also in the coming one, 22 and he subjected all things under his feet and gave him as head over all things to the church, 23 which is his body, the fullness of the one who fills all things in every way."

In this passage, all three spiritual beings of the second choir of angels are mentioned. Paul explicitly affirms that Christ has been resurrected from the dead and elevated to a position of authority at the right hand of God the Father in the heavenly realms. He has been exalted high above the dominations, powers (or virtues as translated by Jerome in his Latin Vulgate), and authorities.

When we look at Scripture, we get a more explicit idea of their role in the Kingdom of Darkness.

As previously mentioned, the Greek term for Dominions, κυριότης, conveys the concept of "lordship," indicating a capacity for ruling. It is reasonable to infer that they continue to exercise dominion over the second choir of angels, albeit now employed in a malevolent cosmic agenda.

Likewise, the Powers operate as "elemental spirits" in the world. Those loyal to Yahweh manifest wondrous phenomena in the cosmos, while the Dark Powers orchestrate formidable events such as natural disasters and similar occurrences.

A parallel scenario applies to the Authorities. Functioning as a warrior class within the Kingdom of Darkness, they have revolted against Yahweh's authority and now operate as renegades within the world.

## The Third Choir

### Principalities

The Bible alludes to fallen principalities and angels, but there is no explicit mention of fallen archangels.

In Colossians 2:13-15, Paul explicitly mentions that Jesus has disarmed the principalities who have seceded from God's Kingdom. He states:

> "13 And Lalthough you were deadJ* in the trespasses and the uncircumcision of your flesh, he made you alive together with him, having forgiven us all our trespasses, 14 having destroyed the certificate of indebtedness in ordinances against us, which was hostile to us, and removed it out of the

way by* nailing it to the cross. 15 When he* had disarmed the principalities and the authorities, he made a display of them in public, triumphing over them by it."

In this passage, the disloyal principalities come into explicit focus. A comprehensive examination of Scripture reveals that these principalities, rather than exercising just rule over humanity, showing compassion to the vulnerable and orphaned, and delivering the oppressed, took an opposing path. Instead of tending to God's people with righteousness, they allowed nations to wander in darkness and became the pagan gods of the nations (Ps. 82:1-8). Notably, the principality (prince) of Greece even engaged in conflict against God's princes (Dan. 10). Such is the modus operandi of dark principalities. They constitute the unseen influences underlying injustice, obscurity, and conflicts among the nations of mankind.

**Angels**

The pages of Scripture reveal a captivating narrative concerning fallen angels, a somber episode echoing the rebellion initiated by their leader, Satan. This descent into defiance is not an isolated incident; rather, it constitutes a recurring motif that threads through the fabric of the biblical narrative.

One remarkable illustration can be discerned in Genesis 6:1-2, where the "sons of God" descend from their celestial abode to engage in illicit unions with human women. This perplexing passage, though often overshadowed by its enigmatic nature, gains clarity through cross-referencing Job 38:7, where the term "sons of God" unambiguously refers to angelic beings.
While some argue that the "sons of God" in Genesis 6 represent the righteous descendants of Seth intermingling with the ungodly lineage of Cain, known as the Sethite interpretation of Genesis 6, this view encounters several challenges.

Firstly, it fails to account for the presence of the Nephilim. How could unions between ordinary humans result in the birth of giants?

Another attempt to explain this passage draws parallels from the Ancient Near East, suggesting that the "sons of God" refer to divinized human rulers who held kingship. However, this approach falters due to the absence of a coherent ancient Near Eastern parallel for a group of divine offspring.

Regarding this, Heiser astutely comments:

> "Ancient parallels restrict divine sonship language to kings. Consequently, the idea of a group of sons of God lacks a coherent ancient Near Eastern parallel. The plural phrase refers to divine beings elsewhere in the Old Testament, not kings (Job 1:6; 2:1; 38:7; Pss. 29:1; 82:6 [cf. 82:1b]; 89:6 [Hebrew: 89:7])." [19]

Further complicating the Sethite interpretation, the text itself does not explicitly label the "sons of God" as descendants of Seth or identify the women as daughters of Cain. Therefore, this view relies on external assumptions not present within the text.

Jude 1:6-7 lends additional weight to the angelic interpretation, condemning the angels who deviated from their rightful domain and engaged in similar misconduct. These transgressions within the angelic realm reverberate through the broader narrative, leaving an indelible imprint on human history, a theme that will be explored further in the upcoming chapter.

---

[19] Michael S. Heiser, *The Unseen Realm: Recovering the Supernatural Worldview of the Bible* (Bellingham, WA; Lexham Press, 2015), 96.

Temporarily setting aside this argument, the Bible presents further instances of fallen angels beyond the Genesis account.

The apostle Paul, in his second letter to the Corinthians (2 Cor. 12), subtly acknowledges the existence of these fallen angels, identifying them as messengers (or angels – angelos in Greek) of Satan. This designation underscores their malevolent nature, aligned with the adversary and actively executing his agenda within the realm of human affairs. This echoes the overarching motif of cosmic conflict, wherein once-loyal beings of light now serve the cause of darkness, harming the followers of God and even disseminating deceitful teachings to unsuspecting individuals.

Historical examples illustrate the manifestation of these fallen influences, with figures like Muhammad and Joseph Smith heralding distorted doctrines under their influence. The Scriptures teach that even if an angel should come and proclaim to us a message that contradicts the Gospel proclaimed they are under a curse (Gal. 1:8).

As we delve into these accounts, a vivid tapestry of fallen angels emerges, depicting their participation in a cosmic rebellion spanning generations. Their defiance, marked by unholy unions and the subversion of divine order, illuminates the intricate interplay between the spiritual and material realms. The Bible's narrative stands as a sobering reminder of the repercussions of disobedience, highlighting the far-reaching impact of fallen beings on the course of human history.

## Conclusion

In the intricate story of the biblical narrative, a profound revelation emerges concerning the unseen realm. Beyond the veil of the material world, a diverse array of spiritual beings exists, both loyal and rebellious, each playing a unique role within the cosmic order.

The exploration of fallen spiritual beings sheds light on the darker undercurrents of this celestial drama. It is within this shadowy domain that we encounter entities that mirror their righteous counterparts, yet stand in stark opposition to Yahweh's divine will. These fallen beings occupy various tiers of the angelic hierarchy, from the lofty heights of cherubim and ophanim to the intricate web of principalities and powers that influence the affairs of nations.

As we journey through the pages of Scripture, we uncover a multifaceted panorama of spiritual realities. The seraphim, once revered and guarding sacred spaces, devolve into beings associated with pagan worship. The cherubim, originally guardians of God's presence, succumb to pride and rebellion, becoming symbols of defiance. Ophanim and thrones, whose fall remains shrouded in mystery, are nevertheless encompassed within Christ's triumphant victory.

The principalities, a diverse cadre of cosmic rulers, showcase a dichotomy between those who serve justice and those who perpetuate darkness. While some uphold divine order, others veer into rebellion and manipulation, becoming malevolent forces that bring about chaos and unrest among humanity.

In this cosmic struggle, even angels, once messengers of light, can be corrupted and led astray by the allure of rebellion. Their deviance brings forth Nephilim, giant beings birthed from forbidden unions who also play a part in the Kingdom of Darkness even until this day.

In essence, the biblical account unveils a portrait of a spiritual conflict that reverberates across the cosmos. It is a tale of loyalty and betrayal, of cosmic forces vying for dominance, and of the ultimate triumph of divine purpose over the forces of darkness. As we ponder these mysteries, we gain a deeper understanding of the unseen realm and its intricate interplay within the overarching narrative of redemption and restoration.

# 3

# Demons

## Introduction

What role do demons play in this intricate web of spiritual beings?

The Bible employs various phrases to describe these malevolent entities. In the New Testament, the terms "evil spirits" or the singular form "evil spirit" are used in reference to them (Matt. 12:45, Luke 7:32, 8:2, 11:26, 19:12-13, 15-16). Additionally, in Matthew 8:32, the Greek term "daimon" (demon) is utilized to refer to an evil spirit. Another expression, "unclean spirit," is also employed to characterize these demons (Matt 10:1, Mark 6:7-13).

Dr. Michael Heiser in his book titled *Demons: What The Bible Really Says About The Powers of Darkness* notes:

> "While the overlap of the terms and phrases is transparent, that the terms are interchanged does not mean that 'unclean spirits' has no special nuance. Whalen has marshaled

evidence that suggests 'unclean spirits' was used in Second Temple Judaism specifically to draw attention to the origin of these evil spirits as the result of an unnatural mixture and the subsequent emergence (and contact with the corpses of the dead Nephilim." [20]

The notion that "demons," "unclean spirits," and "evil spirits" stem from the remains of deceased Nephilim might seem unfamiliar to some. This is primarily due to the prevailing contemporary belief that demons are fallen angels. However, a thorough examination of the data found in the Bible and related literature highlights a different perspective: demons, while originating from fallen angels, are not fallen angels but something different entirely. While this viewpoint might be unfamiliar in our current era, it held significant prevalence in the ancient world.

Throughout Genesis 6 and other passages in the Bible, we confront a startling reality: angelic beings known as the "sons of God" departed from their rightful domain and entered into unions with mortal women (Jude 1:6). This unholy alliance gave rise to a breed of giants known as the Nephilim, who are also referred to

---

[20] Michael S. Heiser, *Demons: What The Bible Really Says About The Powers of Darkness* (Bellingham, WA; Lexham Press, 2020), 196.

by various names in Scripture, such as the "mighty men of renown," "Anakim," and "Rephaim."

**The Nephilim**

The term "Nephilim" in Hebrew translates to "fallen ones." Advocates of the Sethite interpretation of Genesis 6 often cite this term as evidence against the Nephilim being giants. According to this view, the Nephilim are seen as representing the godly lineage of Seth, which "fell" through intermarriage with the ungodly descendants of Cain. This perspective portrays the passage as a cautionary tale about the consequences of the righteous and the unrighteous being unequally yoked.

However, this interpretation faces several significant challenges.

The foremost issue is that it reveals a lack of familiarity with the broader biblical context. While Genesis 6 may not explicitly describe the Nephilim as giants, other passages in the Bible do indeed affirm this connection. A compelling example can be found in Numbers 13:32-33, where we encounter the report given by

Israelite spies who were sent to survey the land and its inhabitants.

> "The land through which we have gone, in spying it out, is a land that devours its inhabitants; and all the people whom we saw in it are men of great size. There also we saw the Nephilim (the sons of Anak are part of the Nephilim), and we became like grasshoppers in our own sight, and so we were in their sight."

While Genesis 6 does not explicitly mention the stature of the Nephilim, it becomes evident from Numbers 13:32-33 that the Israelites associated the Nephilim with giants. This gives us into the worldview of the Israelites and how they would have understood the Genesis 6 narrative. This is also why the reason why the translators of the Greek Septuagint (LXX) translated "nephilim" in Genesis 6 as "giants" or "gigas" in Greek. They were well aware of the lexical usage found in the rest of the Old Testament.

## The Anakim

An intriguing detail in the text is the mention that the "sons of Anak are part of the Nephilim." But who exactly are the sons of Anak? Deuteronomy 1:28 sheds light on this, identifying the sons of Anak as the "Anakim." These individuals are described as "people" who are not only "bigger and taller" than the Israelites but also reside in cities "large and fortified to heaven." Deuteronomy 9:2 further reinforces this, describing the Anakim as "a people great and tall."

In Joshua 11:21-22, we learn that during the Israelite conquest, Joshua successfully eliminated the Anakim from the hill country of Northern Palestine, destroying their cities. Consequently, there were no longer any Anakim in the land, except for those remaining in Gath and Ashdod. Notably, as the biblical narrative unfolds, we encounter the familiar account of David's battle with Goliath from Gath in 1 Samuel 17. Goliath, a giant measuring six cubits and a span, belonged to the Anakim lineage that Joshua had left in Gath.

Thus, the notion that the Nephilim were not giants lacks support. This conclusion can only be reached by isolating Genesis 6 from the broader biblical narrative. The Nephilim are indeed "fallen ones," but not in the demythologized interpretation proposed by those who hold the Sethite view.

Ezekiel in Ezekiel 32:27 refers to the Nephilim as "warriors fallen (נפל) from long ago, who went down to Sheol with their weapons of war, and they placed their sword under their heads, and their shields were on their bones, for the terror of the warriors was in the land of the living."

In essence, the Nephilim are fallen warriors whose spirits descended into the underworld of Sheol, accompanied by their weapons of war. This concept connects with the "Rephaim" data, which further enriches the narrative.

**The Rephaim**

Who were the "Rephaim?"

The term "Rephaim" appears 25 times in the Hebrew Bible. In Deuteronomy 2:9-11, we encounter a narrative about the Israelites' journey through the desert. During this time, the Lord instructed Moses not to antagonize the Moabites, as the land had been given to them as their possession. There, Moses writes:

> "Then the LORD said to me, 'Do not harass Moab, nor provoke them to war, for I will not give you any of their land as a possession, because I have given Ar to the sons of Lot as a possession.' The Emim lived there formerly, a people as great, numerous, and tall as the Anakim. Like the Anakim, they are also regarded as Rephaim, but the Moabites call them Emim."

Here, we see that the Rephaim (or Emim as they were called by the Moabites) were as great and as tall as the Anakim. And like the Anakim, the Emim were regarded as Rephaim.

We actually have in Scripture the story of a Repahaim king named Og. Og was the King of Bashan who was also a giant. Deuteronomy 3:1-11 gives us some more information about him, stating:

"Then we turned, and we went up the road to Bashan, and Og the king of Bashan came out to meet us, he and all of his army for the battle at Edrei. 2 And Yahweh said to me, 'You should not fear him, for I have given him and all of his army and his land into your hand. And so you will do to him as you did to Sihon the king of the Amorites, who was reigning in Heshbon.' 3 And so Yahweh our God also gave Og the king of Bashan, and all of his army into our hand, and we struck him down until not a survivor remained to him. 4 And we captured all of his towns at that time; there was not a city that we did not take from them. 5 All of these were fortified towns with high walls, gates, and bars, ⌊apart from⌋ very many of the villages of the open country. 6 And so we destroyed them just as we had done to Sihon the king of Heshbon; we destroyed utterly each town of males, the women, and the little children. 7 But all of the livestock and the booty of the towns we kept as spoil for ourselves. 8 "And so we took at that time the land from ⌊the control of⌋ the two kings of the Amorites who were ⌊on the other side of the Jordan⌋, from the wadi of Arnon up to ⌊Mount Hermon⌋. 9 (The Sidonians called Hermon 'Sirion,' and the Amorites called it 'Senir.') 10 All of the towns of the plateau and the whole of Gilead and all of Bashan up to Salecah and Edrei, the towns of the kingdom of Og in Bashan. 11 (For only Og, king of Bashan, was left from the remnant of the Rephaim. Indeed, his bedstead—it was a bedstead of iron. It is in Rabbah of the ⌊Ammonites⌋. Nine cubits is its length, and four cubits is its width according to the cubit of a man.)"

Commenting on this, Heiser states:

"For an ancient Israelite reader with command of Hebrew and a worldview that included the idea that supernatural opposition to Israel had something to do with pre-flood events in Mesopotamia, several things in this short passage would have jumped out immediately. None of them are obvious in English translation. First, the most immediate link back to the Babylonian polemic is Og's bed (Hebrew: 'eres). It's dimensions (9x4 cubits) are precisely those of the cultic bed in the ziggurat called Etemenanki — which is the ziggurat most archeologists identify as the Tower of Babel referred to in the Bible. Ziggurats functioned as temples and divine abodes. The unusually large bed at Etemenanki was housed in "the house of the bed (bit erši). It was the place where the god Marduk and his divine wife, Zarpanitu, met annually for ritual lovemaking. Scholars have been struck by the precise correlation. It's hard not to conclude that, as with Genesis 6:1-4, so with Deuteronomy 3, those who put the finishing touches on the Old Testament during the exile in Babylon were connecting Marduk and Og in some way. The most transparent path is in fact giant structure. Og is said to have been the last of the Rephaim — a term connected to the giant Anakim and other ancient giant clans in the Transjordan (Deut. 2:11, 20). Marduk, like other deities in antiquity, was portrayed as superhuman in size. However, the real matrix of ideas in the mind of the biblical author may be derived from wordplay based on Babylonian mythology.

Second, Deuteronomy 3 mentions Og's reign over the city of Edrei (v. 10). Joshua 12:4-5, which looks back on the battle with Og, refers to him as the king of Bashan and living at Ashtaroth and Edrei. These terms — Ashtaroth, Edrei, and Bashan — were theologically loaded terms for an Israelite, and even for their neighbors who worshiped other gods.

Ashtaroth, Edrei, and the Rephaim are mentioned by name in Ugaritic texts. The Rephaim of Ugarit are not described as giants. Rather, they are quasi-divine dead warrior kings who inhabit the underworld."

Here, Heiser brings to light several fascinating insights from the Ancient Near East. In ancient texts from Ugarit, the Rephaim are depicted as quasi-divine dead warrior kings who inhabit the underworld. In other words, the Rephaim are depicted as demi-gods, who are the result of gods and men intermingling. This idea is clearly in sight in Genesis 6 where there are divine sons of God intermingling with the daughters of men and producing the great culture builders – the mighty men of renown. This isn't the only place in the Ancient Near East that this idea comes up.

For example, in *The Epic of Gilgamesh*, Gilgamesh is described as bringing back home a story from before the Flood. He builds walls around the city of Uruk and the holy treasury called the Temple of Heaven. In other words, he was a culture builder and "mighty man of renown" like Nimrod who was also "a mighty one on the earth" (Gen. 10:8 NASB). Interestingly, he is also described as two-thirds god and one-third human. He is also a giant in height, being eighteen feet tall. [21]

---

[21] Sophus Helle, *Gilgamesh: A New Translation of the Ancient Epic* (New Haven, CT; Yale University Press), 3-5.

Just like the Rephaim, he was a giant who was part divine and part human. This was spelled out explicitly during the Second Temple Period in *The Dead Sea Scrolls*. In the scroll called *The Book of Giants (4Q530)*, it says:

> "And all his colleagues entered and Ohiyah explained them what Gilgamesh had told him and Hobabis roared and judgment was pronounced on him. And the guilty cursed the princes, but the giants rejoiced over him and he was cursed again and accepted it. Then two of them dreamed dreams and the sleep of their eyes fled from them . . . And they rose and opened their eyes and they went to Shemihaza, their father. Then he told a story in the congregation of their colleagues, the Nephilim." [22]

Here, Gilgamesh, the mighty semi-divine King of Uruk is mentioned along with the Nephilim and fallen angelic beings mentioned in the Book of Enoch who was a father of the Nephilim named Shemihaza (or spelled Semiaza, who was the ruler of all the angels mentioned in 1 Enoch 6:7-8). Again, this is an Israelite apologetic against certain religious ideas that were present in the

---

[22] Geza Vermes, *The Complete Dead Sea Scrolls in English* (London, England; Penguin Books), 549.

Ancient Near East about gods and the mighty culture builders that were venerated among ancient people.

The second thing that is of interest that Heiser mentions is that the Rephaim in Ancient Ugarit is depicted as "dead warrior kings who inhabit the underworld."

This is the connection point with demons in the Bible. To the surprise of some, we learn that the Bible also speaks of the Rephaim not just as giants, but also as dead warrior kings who inhabit the underworld. As the story of the Bible unfolds, we learn that they have several names that are easy to pass over in English translations. The names they're given in the Bible are "the dead," "departed spirits," and "the shades."

We see David speaking of the Rephaim as "the departed spirits" in Psalm 88:9-13:

> "9 My eye languishes from misery. I call on you, O Yahweh, every day; I spread out my hands to you. 10 Do you work wonders for the dead? Or do the *departed spirits* rise up to praise you? Selah 11 Is your loyal love told in the grave, or your faithfulness *in the underworld*? 12 Are your wonders

known in the darkness, or your righteousness in the land of forgetfulness? 13 But as for me, I cry for help to you, O Yahweh, and in the morning my prayer comes before you."

The Hebrew word for "departed spirits" who are situated in the underworld of Sheol is רְפָאִים or "Rephaim."

Isaiah also speaks of the "dead spirits" in Isaiah 14:9 and 26:14, stating:

9 Sheol below is getting excited over you, to meet ⌊you when you come⌋; it arouses the dead spirits for you, all of the leaders of the earth. It raises all of the kings of the nations from their thrones."

"14 The dead do not live; dead spirits do not rise because you have punished and destroyed them, and you have destroyed all memory of them."

Job also speaks of the "spirits of the dead" who are beneath the waters of the earth who tremble below.

> 5 "The spirits of the dead tremble below the waters and their inhabitants. 6 Sheol is naked before him, and there is no covering for Abaddon

Again, the Hebrew word in all three of these texts for "dead spirits" and "spirits of the dead" is רְפָאִים or "Rephaim."

This is where the notion that "demons," "unclean spirits," and "evil spirits" stem from the remains of deceased Nephilim comes from. "Demons," "unclean spirits," and "evil spirits" in the New Testament are the "spirits of the dead" and "dead spirits" of the Rephaim, who were among the Nephilim clans in the Old Testament. The biblical data couldn't be clearer.

## Other Demonic Entities

In addition to the well-known references to demons in the Bible, there are intriguing passages that allude to other demonic entities, such as Lilit and Azazel, offering further insights into the diverse and enigmatic world of spiritual beings.

**Lilit, Lilitu, and Lilith**

The Night Creature Lilit, often referred to as "Lilith," is a figure associated with the night and darkness. Although not explicitly labeled as a demon in the Bible, ancient Jewish tradition and later interpretations have attributed demonic qualities to her. One of the most commonly cited references is found in Isaiah 34:14:

> "The desert creatures will meet with the wolves, the hairy goat also will cry to its kind; yes, the night monster [Lilit] will settle there and will find herself a resting place."

While the term "Lilit" itself is not present in all translations, the description of a nocturnal creature in this context has led to its identification with a demoness. The association of Lilit with night, wilderness, and unclean places contributed to her characterization as a malevolent entity in various later Jewish writings.

### Azazel

Another notable demonic entity is Azazel. Azazel is mentioned in the Bible as the scapegoat and Goat Demon. The name "Azazel" appears in the context of the Day of Atonement ritual described in Leviticus 16:7-10:

"He shall take the two goats and present them before the Lord at the doorway of the tent of meeting. Aaron shall cast lots for the two goats, one lot for the Lord and the other lot for the scapegoat [Azazel]. Then Aaron shall offer the goat on which the lot for the Lord fell, and make it a sin offering. But the goat on which the lot for the scapegoat [Azazel] fell shall be presented alive before the Lord, to make atonement upon it, to send it into the wilderness as the scapegoat [Azazel]."

The exact nature of Azazel is debated among scholars, but some interpretations suggest a supernatural entity associated with wilderness and desolation. In later Jewish texts, Azazel is often depicted as a demonic figure linked to impurity and sin.

These references to Lilit and Azazel, while sparse, highlight the complexity of spiritual beings in biblical literature. While not as extensively detailed as other entities like demons, they contribute to the rich tapestry of supernatural beings that play roles in ancient religious and cultural contexts. The interpretations and associations surrounding these figures have evolved over time, offering a fascinating glimpse into the ways in which diverse traditions have engaged with and expanded upon the biblical text.

# Conclusion

In the intricate web of spiritual beings within biblical narratives, demons play a distinct role that ties back to the ancient accounts of Nephilim, Anakim, Rephaim, and their connection to fallen angels. While the prevailing contemporary belief is that demons are fallen angels, a closer examination of biblical data and related literature reveals a more nuanced perspective.

The origin of demons is linked to the pre-flood events described in Genesis 6, where angelic beings referred to as the "sons of God" entered unions with mortal women, resulting in the birth of Nephilim, giants of great stature. The biblical narrative and other ancient texts suggest that the Nephilim were not only giants but also powerful warrior kings who held a quasi-divine status, being born from the intermingling of divine and human elements.

The Rephaim, another group of beings mentioned in the Bible, further enrich this narrative. The Rephaim are depicted as deceased warrior kings who inhabit the underworld. They are referred to as "departed spirits," "dead spirits," or "shades" in various biblical passages. This connection between the Rephaim and the spirits of the dead provides insight into the nature of demons, often characterized as evil spirits seeking to harm and possess humans.

This intricate web of spiritual beings, including demons, Nephilim, and Rephaim, demonstrates a complex interplay between divine and human elements, leading to the emergence of malevolent entities that haunt the spiritual realm. The biblical texts offer a unique perspective on the origin and nature of demons, rooted in ancient beliefs and narratives that provide a deeper understanding of these supernatural beings.

**Part Two: Strange Beings From Time & Space**

# 4

# UFO's & UAP

## Introduction

In our modern world, we are surrounded by reports and discussions about UFO and UAP phenomena. However, for Christians, this raises an important question: how should we approach and consider these phenomena in light of our faith?

Many Christians tend to dismiss the significance of UFO and UAP phenomena by categorizing them as fabricated or unreal. Others within the Christian community propose an alternative perspective, suggesting that these unidentified aerial objects are simply demons. In this chapter, I aim to present an alternative viewpoint that departs from both of these stances. This theory advocates for more serious consideration of UFO and UAP data, while avoiding the tendency to hastily dismiss them as mere manifestations of demons.

## The Religiosity of UFO & UAP Phenomena

To delve into this subject, it's important to begin with an intriguing observation made by journalist and ufologist John Keel. Keel highlighted an intriguing pattern within UFO and UAP phenomena, particularly noting its consistent alignment with religious interpretations until the year 1848.

Keel's insight reveals that a religious context frequently framed the phenomenon until technological advancements altered the landscape. Gray Barker, reflecting on Keel's observation, elaborates:

> "As man's technology improved, and many religious beliefs were discarded, the phenomenon was obliged to update its manifestations and establish a new frame of reference. The phantom armies and angels so frequently reported in the past were replaced by transmogrifications that appeared to match man's own technological achievements." [23]

In essence, historical encounters with "lights in the sky" were religious in nature. What's remarkable about this observation is that Keel discerned it was not individuals imposing a religious framework onto their extraterrestrial experiences, but rather the

---

[23] John A. Keel and Andrew B. Colvin, *Flying Saucer To The Center Of Your Mind: Selected Writings of John A. Keel* (Seattle, WA; Metadisc Books and The Seattle Conceptual Art Museum 2013), 19.

UFO and UAP phenomena itself that incorporated the religious frame of reference into its manifestations. It wasn't until man advanced technologically and cast aside his religious beliefs that the phenomena's "mask" changed. The UFO's and UAP transmogrified and took on the elements associated with the phenomena to this day.

Because of this, Jacques Valée who is a world-renowned astrophysicist, astronomer, and computer scientist states that:

> "This being the case, the development of a new myth feeding upon this duality is entirely predictable. In the absence of a rational solution to the mystery, and public interest in the matter being intense, it is quite likely that in the coming years, every new brand of charlatanism will use it as a base, although it is not possible to predict its exact form. We may very well be living the early years of a new mythological movement, and it may eventually give our technological age its Olympus, its fairyland, or its Walhalla, whether we regard such a development as an asset or blow to our culture." [24]

---

[24] Jacques Valée, Passport to Magonia: From Folklore to Flying Saucers, 150.

Valée's cautionary words, initially penned in 1969, have undeniably manifested in our present times. The contributions of contemporary proponents of the Ancient Astronaut Theory, such as Zecharia Sitchin and Eric von Däniken, align with the idea that civilizations of antiquity revered ancient aliens. Similarly, the endeavors of Dr. Steven Greer have revolved around the pursuit of close encounters of the 5th kind (CE-5) through the application of transcendental meditation techniques.

It is evident that Valée's concerns about the potential manipulation of human belief systems through the lens of extraterrestrial interactions have not only persisted but have been accentuated by these modern developments. The notions propagated by Sitchin and von Däniken advocate for a reinterpretation of historical accounts as interactions with alien entities, offering a perspective that can subtly reshape established religious and cultural paradigms.

Furthermore, Dr. Greer's pursuit of CE-5 experiences through meditative practices underscores the contemporary fascination with establishing contact with extraterrestrial intelligences. While these pursuits might emerge from a desire for peaceful interaction, they also accentuate the vulnerability of human consciousness to manipulation and distortion, harkening back to Valée's original apprehensions.

As we navigate these intricate realms of theory and practice, it becomes essential to engage with these ideas critically and maintain an awareness of their potential implications for our understanding of history, culture, and spirituality. Valée's prescient warning continues to serve as a reminder of the multifaceted impact that beliefs in extraterrestrial phenomena can exert on humanity and collective consciousness.

## The Mask

So, what can we deduce from the labyrinth of UFO and UAP phenomena? As I delve into this realm, let me assert from the outset that I am inclined to believe in the authenticity of the contactee literature. John Keel's observations illuminate a diverse spectrum of encounters, ranging from trance-like states and hypnotism to hallucinations, distortions of reality, astral projection, and encounters with cosmic and false illumination. The connection points between contactees from differing places and times are too much to overlook.

However, my perspective diverges from the notion that UFOs and UAPs directly represent extraterrestrial entities originating from distant realms in space, that they embody alien gods worshiped by ancient civilizations, or that they're simply demons. Instead, I propose an alternative interpretation.

Drawing from the scriptural data we've explored thus far, I contend that the phenomenon of UFOs and UAPs can be linked to the "sons of God" mentioned in biblical texts like Genesis 6 when we compare the biblical, UFO, and UAP data. This perspective offers a unique lens through which to examine these modern encounters.

In this framework, the concept of "extraterrestrial" becomes less a geographical marker and more a manifestation of beings that transcend conventional understandings of space and time. The intricate blend of technological manifestations and psychological experiences witnessed in UFO and UAP encounters could be a modern façade for the enigmatic beings that have traversed the boundaries between the divine and the earthly throughout history.

**Flying Saucers, Advanced Technology, and Biologics**

Over the past several years, a fresh wave of understanding has graced our comprehension of UFO and UAP craft. In 2020, the veil was partially lifted as the US Department of Defense (DOD) declassified three Navy videos— one hailing from November 2004 and two from January 2015. Notably, the November 2004 footage has earned the moniker "tic tac" video. [25]

On that particular day, the Nimitz Carrier Strike Group was immersed in a training exercise just off the California coast, approximately 100 miles southwest of San Diego. Aboard the USS Princeton, a Navy vessel integral to the training ensemble, operators witnessed "multiple anomalous aerial vehicles" descending from 80,000 feet to nearly nothing in a split second, as discerned by advanced radar. Taking the helm of the investigation were David Fravor, a retired Navy Commander of the F/A-18F squadron on the USS Nimitz, and Leuitnent Commander Alex Dietrich.

These two aviators, accompanied by weapons system officers in the back seat of their F/A-18Fs, were eyewitnesses to a truly extraordinary sight—a "little white 'Tic Tac'-looking object just above the whitewater area." This unconventional spectacle

---

[25] See the Department of Defense's statement here:
https://www.defense.gov/News/Releases/Release/Article/2165713/statement-by-the-department-of-defense-on-the-release-of-historical-navy-videos/

persisted for approximately five minutes. As Fravor endeavored to approach the enigma, the "Tic Tac" demonstrated an eerie synchronicity with his movements, indicating a startling degree of awareness. Astonishingly, the object was on par in size with Fravor's F/A-18F, yet bore no markings, wings, or exhaust plumes. When Fravor attempted to intercept the UAP, it defied conventional understanding by accelerating at an astonishing rate, vanishing from sight and reappearing roughly 60 miles away within a mere minute.

Fravor's testimonies underscore the perplexity of the situation. The "Tic Tac" defied the limits of our understanding of material science, surpassing present capabilities and seemingly prognosticating advancements of the next decade or two. His insights have garnered further credibility as he offered sworn testimony before Congress, addressing the incident with gravitas.

Simultaneously, in the same congressional hearing, David Grusch, a former intelligence officer representing two Pentagon task forces that investigated UAPs, came forward as a whistleblower. Under oath, he imparted to the House Oversight Committee's national security subcommittee a staggering revelation—an ongoing "multi-decade UAP crash retrieval and reverse-engineering program." In addition, he conveyed that he had personally interacted with officials privy to craft with "non-human" origins and revealed that "biologics" had been retrieved from some of these enigmatic vehicles.

In light of these unprecedented disclosures, a pivotal question emerges: What interpretation should we ascribe to these extraordinary craft and their advanced technological capabilities that feature prominently in UFO and UAP sightings?

Keel offers an interesting perspective on UFO craft and hardware that has been recovered. He notes:

> "There is absolutely no evidence that UFOs are extraterrestrial or interplanetary in nature. All substances and 'hardware' alleged to have come from UFOs have been composed of earthly materials." [26]

Dr. Michael Heiser also raises this same point as well about UFO craft, suggesting that we're not dealing with extraterrestrials.

---

[26] John A. Keel and Andrew B. Colvin, *Flying Saucer To The Center Of Your Mind: Selected Writings of John A. Keel* (Seattle, WA; Metadisc Books and The Seattle Conceptual Art Museum 2013), 37.

> "UFO descriptions evolve over time with technological change. That's one good reason to conclude we aren't dealing with alien visitors. Think about it. If aliens were really visiting the planet during the last 100 years, would their craft really evolve from propeller-powered dirigibles to anti-gravity? Wouldn't they have had the latter already?" [27]

How then should we interpret such a statement, particularly considering Grusch's sworn testimony about the retrieval of crafts of "non-human" origin and the presence of "biologics"?

In my view, it is highly plausible that the retrieved crafts are created by entities that are not of human origin. Furthermore, I am convinced that there is ample reason to believe that non-human "biologics" have also been obtained. This conviction stems from my observation that when the gathered data is juxtaposed with biblical accounts, a compelling case can be made that the "non-human" entities responsible for the crafts and biologics align closely with the biblical concept of the sons of God.

When we look at the data of the sons of God in the Bible and in the literature of the Second Temple Period, we clearly see

---

[27] https://drmsh.com/ufo-descriptions-evolve-time-technological-change/

celestial beings who are not bound by human limitations and who seem to have a connection with technology.

In 1 Enoch 8:1-3, we see that the fallen angels in the Genesis 6 account give lessons to humans about how to utilize different technologies.

> "Azael taught the humans to make swords, weapons, shields, and breastplates – the lessons of the angels; and they showed them their mining and craftsmanship, anklets and adornment, powers and painted eyes, and all kinds of choice stones and dying. Much ungodliness and prostitution happened, and they were led astray and ruined in all their ways. Semiaza taught enchantments and cutting of roots; Armaros, spells of healing; Rhakiel, astrology; Chochiel, the science of symptoms; Sathiel, watching the stars; Seriel, the course of the moon."

Within this text, we encounter a connection point linking the fallen angels, known as the sons of God, to the dissemination of advanced knowledge in weapon forging, mining, craftsmanship, jewelry, enchantments, herbology, and astrology. In the context of the Second Temple Period, it was commonly believed that these various technologies found their origins with the fallen watchers described in Genesis 6.

For us, living in a technologically advanced world, these skills might not immediately appear as groundbreaking technology. However, to those who lived in centuries past, these capabilities would have undoubtedly been perceived as highly advanced.

But what about the concept of "biologics"? Aren't angels traditionally considered to be purely spiritual beings?

There is a case to be made that angels may have bodies. While angels are commonly thought of as purely spiritual beings, various passages in religious texts suggest the possibility of them having the ability to take on corporeal forms.

In the Bible, there are instances where angels appear to humans in physical forms. For instance, in the story of Abraham and the three visitors in Genesis 18, the visitors are referred to as "men" and are described as eating and conversing with Abraham. Similarly, in the story of Lot and the angels in Genesis 19, the angels are also described as men who eat. These instances imply a material presence rather than a purely spiritual one.

## Luminous Like The Stars

The sons of God explanation also gives explanatory power to the luminosity associated with UFO and UAP phenomena.

Colvin notes that one of the two major kinds of UFO phenomena involves "intelligent lights," orbs," and "energy balls." [28] Barker also notes the cockpits of UAP being "brilliantly illuminated (a distinct abnormality, for such would interfere with pilot vision." [29]

In the Bible, the sons of God are presented as luminous beings who are like the stars. Job writes of the sons of God being like the morning stars in Job 38:4-7.

> "Where were you at my laying the foundation of the earth? Tell me, if you possess understanding. 5 Who determined its measurement? Yes, you do know. Or who stretched the measuring line upon it? 6 On what were its bases sunk? Or who laid its cornerstone, 7 when the morning stars were singing together and all the sons of God shouted for joy?"

---

[28] John A. Keel and Andrew B. Colvin, *Flying Saucer To The Center Of Your Mind: Selected Writings of John A. Keel* (Seattle, WA; Metadisc Books and The Seattle Conceptual Art Museum 2013), 15.

[29] Ibid, 19.

Heiser comments on the "star language" used in reference to the sons of God, noting:

> "Since the members of God's heavenly host are referred to as "heavenly ones," it should come as no surprise that they are also called "stars" (kōkeḇîm). Indeed, the very designation "host" draws on descriptions of celestial bodies in the Old Testament (e.g., Gen 2:1; Jer 8:2): The identification of personified stars with angels of the heavenly hosts is well accepted within a totally monotheistic religious system: the stars stand in God's presence, to the right and the left of His throne (1 Kgs 22:19; 2 Chr 18:18); they serve Him (Ps 103:21; Neh 9:6).... At the head of the heavenly hosts stands a "Prince of the army" (Josh 5:14–15; Dan 8:11), probably the highest star and the farthest from the earth, even if the actual leader is God, to whom the starry army belongs. From this conception derives the syntagm "Lord/God of hosts" (Yhwh ʾĕlōhê ṣĕbāʾôt) occurring in numerous biblical passages. Perhaps the most familiar passage in this regard is Job 38:5–7, where God asks Job: Who determined [the earth's] measurements—surely you know! Or who stretched the line upon it? On what were its bases sunk, or who laid its cornerstone, when the morning

stars sang [kōkebê bōqer] together and all the sons of God shouted for joy? As we'll note later in our discussion, "sons of God" is a term for the divine members of God's divine family-entourage. The heavenly sons of God who watched the creation of the earth are described as "morning stars." In Isaiah 14:13, the hubris of the king of Babylon is analogized with that of a rebel who sought to displace the God of heaven: "I will ascend to heaven; above the stars of God [kōkebê ʾēl] I will set my throne on high." Scholars have long known that these lines in Isaiah 14 draw on a tale of divine rebellion present in Ugaritic texts, where the gods of El's council are referred to as the "assembly of the stars [kkbm]." The point of star language for divine members of the heavenly host should be obvious. The members of Yahweh's host are not of earth. They are celestial, transcendent beings whose home is in the heavenly realm, the abode of God." [30]

This connection point demands careful consideration. The luminance of UAP cockpits raises intriguing questions about their nature, potentially indicating that these craft could serve as terrestrial camouflage for something more mysterious. This notion aligns with observations made by Keel, who suggested that a

---

[30] Michael S. Heiser, *Angels: What the Bible Really Says about God's Heavenly Host* (Bellingham, WA: Lexham Press, 2018), 8–10.

significant portion of these craft might be transient and manufactured as earthly facades to obscure the genuine phenomenon at play.[31]

## Hypnosis and Trances

This perspective also provides a framework to explain the hypnotic and trance-like states frequently reported by contactees.

As the biblical narrative unfolds, a parallel can be drawn between the sons of God and the deities worshipped by various nations. This connection emerges from the rebellion of certain members within Yahweh's divine council, who assume the titles of gods in defiance of their original role.

In Deuteronomy 32:8, we are granted insight into this event. The passage sheds light on the events that unfolded when Yahweh dispersed the nations during the events at Babel. As the nations were scattered and their boundaries defined, a significant change occurred. Due to their rebellion, Yahweh disinherited them and appointed angelic mediators—the sons of God—as intermediaries. The verse states:

---

[31] John A. Keel and Andrew B. Colvin, *Flying Saucer To The Center Of Your Mind: Selected Writings of John A. Keel* (Seattle, WA; Metadisc Books and The Seattle Conceptual Art Museum 2013), 20.

> "When the Most High apportioned the nations, at his dividing up of the sons of humankind, he fixed the boundaries of the peoples, according to the number of the sons of God."

These angelic mediators were designated to act as intermediaries between the nations and Yahweh. Although this concept might seem unfamiliar to us, it aligns with the dynamics of disinheriting someone from a family. In such instances, communication typically takes place through intermediaries or mediators when direct interaction is no longer possible.

As the biblical narrative progresses, we learn that this particular group of angelic intermediaries also rebelled against Yahweh just as the sons of God in Genesis 6 did.

In Psalm 82, we catch a glimpse of Yahweh stepping into the midst of the gods of the nations and proclaiming judgment upon them, vowing to one day re-inherit the nations because they had led them into darkness. The text states:

> "1 God stands in the divine assembly; he administers judgment in the midst of the gods. 2 "How long will you judge unjustly and ⌊show favoritism to the wicked⌋? Selah 3 Judge

on behalf of the helpless and the orphan; provide justice to the afflicted and the poor. 4 Rescue the helpless and the needy; deliver them from the hand of the wicked." 5 They do not know or consider. They go about in the darkness, so that all the foundations of the earth are shaken. 6 I have said, "You are gods, and sons of the Most High, all of you. 7 However, you will die like men, and you will fall like one of the princes." 8 Rise up, O God, judge the earth, because you shall inherit all the nations."

This passage offers insight into the actions of the sons of God while ruling as gods over the nations. They perpetuated injustice by favoring the wicked and neglecting the vulnerable—the helpless, the orphan, the afflicted, and the poor. Their failure to protect the weak and deliver them from wickedness led to the nations being immersed in ignorance and darkness.

Furthermore, historical examination reveals parallels in religious practices during the reign of the sons of God as gods of the nations. Interestingly, these connections also intersect with the phenomena of UFOs, UAPs, hypnotism, and trances.

From the latter part of the 7th century B.C. to the 4th century A.D., the Temple of the god Apollo in Delphi held a central role within the Greco-Roman world. This temple was the "navel of the world" for Greeks and was central to seeking divine guidance, particularly among kings seeking revelations from the gods.

The manner in which these revelations were obtained is particularly intriguing. Within the temple complex of the temple, a priestess known as Pythia occupied the role of oracle. When kings sought guidance, the Pythia would venture into the sacred inner chamber referred to as the "mantic bay." There, she would undergo a state of possession by the god Apollo, entering a hypnotic, trance-like state through which she would convey divine revelations.

This practice illustrates an intriguing parallel to the concept of hypnotic and trancelike states associated with both the ancient oracle and certain aspects of UFO and UAP phenomena. The connection between altered states of consciousness, otherworldly experiences, and communication with higher entities is a fascinating thread that runs through various cultures and periods of history.

## Sexual Contact

The final link that warrants exploration pertains to sexual interactions. Within a significant portion of contactee literature, references to sexual contact are prevalent. Keel observes this phenomenon, expressing:

> "There is a well-known historic phenomenon that has been heavily documented for centuries and has involved thousands of people both male and female. This phenomenon involved the appearance of nonhuman entities that seduce and have sexual intercourse with their victims. . . One weird case is fully described in a book titled UFO Warning, by New Zealander John Steward. He became obsessed with the UFO phenomenon in the early 1950s and was assisted in his research by an attractive young lady he calls 'Barbara." After having some close-up UFO sightings in 1954 and receiving anonymous, threatening phone calls ordering them to discontinue their UFO studies, Barbara claimed that she returned home one night to find a foul odor in her apartment. Then she was brutally attacked by a creature she could not see. She said that it had skin the

texture of sandpaper. It raped her and left her body covered with small scratches." [32]

This account is undeniably unsettling. It should cause us to pause and engage this topic with profound contemplation. What kind of entity could engage in such acts?

Once again, the supernatural narrative depicted in the Bible provides a compelling framework for understanding these perplexing accounts. Genesis 6 recounts the interaction between celestial beings known as the sons of God and mortal women, resulting in a significant intertwining of realms. This narrative also has a parallel within the literature of the Second Temple Period, where interpretations of this account delve further into the dynamics at play, including the disturbing theme of the mistreatment of women in prostitution (1 Enoch 8:2).

## Conclusion

Navigating the realm of UFO and UAP phenomena while considering their implications for Christian faith and understanding is a task that requires careful analysis and open-minded inquiry.

---

[32] John A. Keel and Andrew B. Colvin, *The Book of Mothman: Everything You Wanted To Know About Reality Distortions But Were Afraid To Ask* (Point Pleasant, WV; New Saucerian Books 2015), 141.

The interpretations presented herein diverge from the extremes of outright dismissal and demonization, offering an alternative viewpoint that encourages a deeper examination of these phenomena.

The observation that UFO and UAP phenomena have historically embraced a religious context until the advent of technological advancements underscores the complexity of these encounters. This pattern aligns with the insights of journalist John Keel and the subsequent shift from overtly religious manifestations to manifestations that parallel technological progress. This transformation invites us to view UFO and UAP phenomena as more than random occurrences but rather as phenomena intricately intertwined with technological and spiritual shifts.

Jacques Valée's warning about the potential manipulative influence of extraterrestrial beliefs on human culture is particularly pertinent in the modern context. The popularity of Ancient Astronaut Theory and the pursuit of contact experiences through meditation techniques like CE-5 underscores the capacity of these beliefs to reshape cultural narratives and belief systems, potentially leading to devastating consequences.

It is essential to approach this information with discernment and critical thinking. The belief that UFOs and UAPs are direct representatives of extraterrestrial entities originating from faraway planets, or simply demons, may be overly simplistic. Instead, by connecting the dots between biblical narratives and modern UFO and UAP data, we can propose an alternative interpretation.

This perspective suggests that UFOs and UAPs are not necessarily interstellar travelers, but rather entities that traverse the boundaries between the earthly and the divine. The technological displays witnessed in these encounters may be modern manifestations of the ancient celestial beings described as the sons of God in biblical texts. The accounts of advanced knowledge, including weapon making, craftsmanship, and healing arts, attributed to these beings align with the UFO and UAP phenomenon, suggesting a possible connection.

The luminous appearances of UFOs and UAPs find resonance in the description of the sons of God as beings "like the morning stars." The suggestion that angels may assume corporeal forms further adds credibility to the idea that these entities could be linked to the luminous phenomena.

The hypnotic and trance-like states reported by contactees and their historical counterparts, such as the oracle of Delphi, can also be understood within this framework. The parallel between altered states of consciousness and communication with higher beings resonates with the ancient practice of obtaining divine guidance through similar methods.

Lastly, the unsettling accounts of sexual encounters in contactee literature and their alignment with biblical narratives shed light on a troubling aspect of the phenomena. The suggestion that these encounters may be linked to celestial beings aligns with ancient descriptions of celestial sons of God engaging with humanity.

In conclusion, exploring UFO and UAP phenomena through this multifaceted lens offers an alternative perspective that bridges the gap between ancient beliefs and modern experiences. While this interpretation raises thought-provoking questions and challenges conventional understanding, it also calls for responsible and balanced engagement. Balancing critical analysis with an open-minded approach allows us to consider these phenomena with the gravity they deserve while preserving the integrity of both our faith and our pursuit of truth.

# 5

# Cryptids

## Introduction

In today's modern landscape, our attention is not only drawn to discussions and reports concerning UFO and UAP phenomena but also to an array of sightings involving strange and mythic creatures. These sightings span a spectrum, encompassing everything from mothmen to sirens, fairies, and a multitude of other intriguing entities. Yet, for those who adhere to the Christian faith, a significant question emerges: How should we navigate and interpret these phenomena within the context of our beliefs, especially when we see that contact with these kinds of entities goes back centuries to even Christian witnesses?

Just as with UFO and UAP phenomena, many Christians tend to downplay the significance of cryptid phenomena, brushing them off as mere fabrications or unreal tales. Some may casually wave their hands and label them as "myths and folklore," relegating them to meaninglessness. On the other hand, some members of the Christian community offer an alternative interpretation, suggesting that these mythic creatures are synonymous with demons. However, the intention of this chapter is to diverge from both of these perspectives. Within these pages, I endeavor to present an alternative viewpoint that calls for a more earnest consideration of the realm of cryptids. The goal is to move beyond hasty dismissals, whether as mere fabrications or demonic manifestations and delve into a nuanced exploration of these intriguing phenomena.

## The Secret Commonwealth

The initial phenomenon under our investigation is that of fairies. However, it's important to clarify that the fairies discussed here are not the whimsical and child-like creatures commonly portrayed in Disney movies.

Between 1691-1692, Scottish Minister and Folklorist Robert Kirk wrote about these enigmatic beings in his classic book titled *The Secret Commonwealth of Elves, Fauns, and Fairies*. There, he spoke of these creatures saying:

> "These Siths or Fairies they call Sleagh Maith or the Good People [...] are said to be of middle nature between Man and Angel, as were Daemons thought to be of old; of intelligent fluidous Spirits, and light changeable bodies (like those called Astral) somewhat of the nature of a condensed cloud, and best seen in twilight. These bodies be so pliable through the subtlety of Spirits that agitate them, that they can make them appear or disappear at pleasure." [33]

In the eyes of the ancient Celtic people, fairies were believed to possess "subtle bodies" capable of assuming diverse forms that could influence the natural elements around them. Strikingly, these entities were often identified with the deities of pagan Ireland – the *Tuatha De Danān*, a connection that led some to draw parallels with fallen angels. This notion was eloquently addressed by W.B. Yeats, who remarked:

> "The Irish word for fairy is *sheehogue* [sidheóg], a diminutive of "shee" in *banshee*. Fairies are *deenee shee* [daoine sidhe] (fairy people). Who are they? "Fallen angels who were not good enough to be saved, nor bad enough to be lost," say the peasantry. "The gods of the earth," says the Book of

---
[33] Robert Kirk, *The Secret Commonwealth of Elves, Fauns, and Fairies* (Orlando, FL; Anados Books 2018), 31.

Armagh. "The gods of pagan Ireland," say the Irish antiquarians, "the *Tuatha De Danān*," who, when no longer worshipped and fed with offerings, dwindled away in the popular imagination, and now are only a few spans high." And they will tell you, in proof, that the names of fairy chiefs are the names of old Danān heroes, and the places where they especially gather together, Danān burying-places, and that the Tuatha De Danān used also to be called the *slooa-shee* [sheagh sidhe] (the fairy host), or *Marcha shee* (the fairy cavalcade). . . Are they "the gods of the earth?" Perhaps! Many poets, and all mystic and occult writers, in all ages and countries, have declared that behind the visible are chains on chains of conscious beings, who are not of heaven but of the earth, who have no inherent form, but change according to their whim, or the mind that sees them. You cannot lift your hand without influencing and being influenced by hoards. The visible world is merely their skin." [34]

It's worth highlighting that Yeats' depiction of fairies strikingly aligns with the biblical concept of elemental spirits (stoicheia). As previously explored, the Bible elucidates the existence of

---

[34] W.B. Yeats, *Irish Folk and Fairy Tales* (New York, NY; Chartwell Books 2015), 22-23.

imperceptible angelic entities intertwined with the fundamental elements of the observable universe. Remarkably, Yeats' perspective resonates with Celtic belief, albeit employing the term "fairies" instead of angels. In the Celtic cosmology, these entities similarly occupied a presence within the world, exerting influence upon the visible realm that served as a tangible manifestation of their presence. This interplay between the seen and unseen realms was a shared perspective, linking biblical and Celtic understandings through the lens of these enigmatic entities.

Another significant point of convergence arises from Yeats' insight that fairies were also perceived as the pagan deities of Ireland, specifically the Tuatha De Danān. This parallel serves as another link between Celtic and biblical narratives. Delving into the question of who these enigmatic figures were, we find our exploration leads us to the ancient Celtic text known as Lebor Gabála Érenn (The Book of Invasions). Within this chronicle, we gain insight into the enigmatic beings that embarked on a noteworthy incursion into the Celtic lands.

> "§55. So that they were the Tuatha De Danann who came to Ireland. In this wise they came, in dark clouds. They landed on the mountains of Conmaicne Rein in Connachta; and

they brought a darkness over the sun for three days and three nights. §56. They demanded battle of kingship of the Fir Bolg. A battle was fought between them, to wit the first battle of Mag Tuired, in which a hundred thousand of the Fir Bolg fell. Thereafter they [the TDD] took the kingship of Ireland. Those are the Tuatha Dea - gods were their men of arts, non-gods their husbandmen. They knew the incantations of druids, and charioteers, and trappers, and cupbearers. §57. It is the Tuatha De Danann who brought with them the Great Fal, [that is, the Stone of Knowledge], which was in Temair, whence Ireland bears the name of "The Plain of Fal." He under whom it should utter a cry was King of Ireland; until Cu Chulainn smote it, for it uttered no cry under him nor under his fosterling, Lugaid, son of the three Finds of Emain. And from that out the stone uttered no cry save under Conn of Temair. Then its heart flew out from it [from Temair] to Tailltin, so that is the Heart of Fal which is there. It was no chance which caused it, but Christ's being born, which is what broke the powers of the idols." [35]

Notice here the convergence among the narratives found in the Celtic *Lebor Gabála Érenn*, Genesis 6, and 1 Enoch 6-8, where

---

[35] *Lebor Gabála Érenn: Book of the Taking of Ireland Part 1-5.* ed. and tr. by R. A. S. Macalister. Dublin: Irish Texts Society, 1941.

notable points of connection surface. Celestial entities descend from the celestial realm and alight upon significant mountains—Mount Hermon in the case of 1 Enoch and the mountains of Conmaicne Rein as detailed in "Lebor Gabála Érenn." Furthermore, these beings are associated with the transmission of esoteric knowledge, accompanied by advanced technologies.

To our modern sensibilities, steeped in a world of disenchantment, the notion of fairy gods might appear whimsical or even foolish. However, for the people inhabiting these ancient lands, there existed a profound understanding that these beings held significant sway. The perspective of these cultures underscores that these entities were regarded as tangible forces demanding genuine consideration. So much so, that it even played into the ecclesiastical life of these people.

Kirk writing from Scotland astutely observed the intricate movements of the fairies and their palpable impact on the lives of the people. He said:

> "They remove to other lodgings at the beginning of each quarter of the year, so traversing till doomsday, being

impotent of staying in one place, and finding some ease by journeying and changing habitations. Their chameleon-like bodies swim in the air near the earth with bag and baggage: and at such revolution of time, seers, or men of the second sight (females being seldom so qualified) have very terrifying encounters with them, even on high ways; who therefore usually shun to travel abroad at these four seasons of the year, and thereby have made it a custom to this day among the Scottish-Irish to keep church duly every first Sunday of the quarter to sene or hallow themselves, their corns and cattle, from the shots and stealth of these wandering tribes; and many of these superstitious people will not be seen in church again till the next quarter begins, as if no duty were to be learned or done by them, but all the Use of Worship and Sermons were to save them from the arrows that fly in the dark." [36]

Writing from Ireland, Yeats echoed very similar sentiments, noting stating:

"They have three great festivals in the year – May Eve, Midsummer Eve, November Eve. On May Eve, every

---
[36] Robert Kirk, *The Secret Commonwealth of Elves, Fauns, and Fairies* (Orlando, FL; Anados Books 2018), 32.

seventh year, they fight all around, but mostly on the Plain-a-Bawn, for the harvest, for the best hearts of grain belong to them. An old man told me he saw them fight once; they tore the thatch off a house in the midst of it all. Had anyone else been near they would merely have seen a great wind whirling everything into the air as it passed. When the wind makes the straws and leaves while as it passes, that is the fairies, and the peasantry take off their hats and say, "God bless them." [37]

Within this cultural milieu, a prevailing belief emerges that specific periods of the year hold heightened activity for these ethereal entities. Kirk alluded to quarterly cycles, while Yeats echoes the notion in three out of four quarters. What proves intriguing is the reversal of roles in perceptions of superstition. It is not those who acknowledge the existence of these angelic fae or take prudent measures to avert encounters who are deemed superstitious. Rather, the label falls upon those who, in their belief that attending church only once per quarter can shield them from the enchantments of these beings.

---

[37] W.B. Yeats, *Irish Folk and Fairy Tales* (New York, NY; Chartwell Books 2015), 23.

Interestingly, this fairy-lore also found its way to other countries as well. For example, when the Scots-Irish settled in the United States, particularly in West Virginia, they brought their angelic fae with them across the Atlantic.

Miners in the mountains of Appalachia still to this day talk about "blue caps," which were fairies that inhabit mines and appear as small blue flames. Many miners leave food offerings for the blue caps and believe that if they treat them with respect, they will lead them to coal deposits and forewarn of mine cave-ins or deadly gasses.

Could there be a concealed realm, a secret commonwealth of fairies, intricately intertwined with the tapestry of creation, veiling themselves within the very elements of the world? It appears so, and intriguingly, the Bible employs terms such as elemental spirits, powers, or virtues to describe entities that parallel this notion.

## Mothman

Speaking of West Virginia, it's worth delving into another enigmatic figure that roams the hills of this region—the infamous Mothman of Point Pleasant.

The Mothman phenomenon stands as a captivating example of high strangeness which captures attention for multiple reasons. What particularly sets it apart is the sheer number of witnesses and the overwhelming surge of inexplicable occurrences that accompanied this event, which climaxed with the collapse of the Silver Bridge.

Keele summarizes the beginning of the Mothman saga, stating:

> "Around midnight on November 15, 1966, two young married couples, Mr. and Mrs. Roger Scarbertty and Mr. and Mrs. Steve Mallette, were driving through an abandoned WWII ammunition dump known as the TNT area, seven miles outside of Pt. Pleasant, West Virginia, when they unwittingly entered the Twilight Zone. As they passed an old deserted power plant, they saw a weird figure standing beside the road staring at them. 'It was shaped like a man, but bigger,' Roger Scarberry told me. 'Maybe six-and-a-half or seven feet tall. And it had big wings folded against its back.' 'But it was those eyes that got us,' Mrs. Scarberry declared with a shudder. 'It had two big, red eyes, like automobile tail-light reflectors.' 'For a minute we could only stare at it,' Roger

said. 'Then it just turned and sort of shuffled toward the open door of the old power plant. We didn't wait around.' Roger, a strapping but soft-spoken and introspective 19-yr. old, stepped on the gas pedal of his souped-up jalopy and headed out of the TNT Area for Rt. 62, which leads into Point Pleasant. As they shot down the highway, his wife cried out, 'It's following us!' 'We were doing better than 100 miles per hour,' Roger said. All four swore that 'the bird' was low overhead, its wings spread out to about 10 feet. It seemed to keep up with the car effortlessly, even though its wings weren't flapping."[38]

Keel notes that this was not an isolated incident. Over 100 people in Ohio and West Virginia had seen this creature since November 1966. Many of the witnesses were very credible, including schoolteachers, businessmen, pilots, and members of the National Guard.

Amidst the mysterious aura of the Mothman phenomena, a pervasive wave of strangeness swept across the Point Pleasant area, leaving behind a trail of bewildering events that further blurred the lines between the ordinary and the extraordinary. The

---

[38] John A. Keel and Andrew B. Colvin, *The Book of Mothman: Everything You Wanted To Know About Reality Distortions But Were Afraid To Ask* (Point Pleasant, WV; New Saucerian Books 2015), Pg.

sightings of the winged creature were not isolated occurrences; rather, they were intertwined with a tapestry of anomalies that defied explanation.

An unsettling connection emerged as some individuals who had encountered the Mothman found themselves diagnosed with "eye burn" or conjunctivitis, adding a peculiar layer of physicality to the already mystifying encounters. The very act of witnessing this creature seemed to have tangible consequences.

As if choreographed by an unseen hand, the stage was set for a convergence of otherworldly phenomena. The skies above Point Pleasant witnessed an uptick in UFO activity, painting the night canvas with lights and forms that confounded the rational mind. In a March 1967 encounter, a resident from Ohio recounted a chilling pursuit by a "huge winged something" as it trailed his vehicle, an event that seemingly defied the laws of physics and known reality.

The intertwining of the Mothman with UFO sightings reached another level of intrigue when two witnesses reported an astonishing sight on May 19, 1967 – the Mothman ascending to meet a UFO. This apparent interaction between the winged creature and unidentified aerial objects only deepened the enigma, beckoning us to question whether these phenomena were connected by an unseen thread that spanned dimensions beyond our understanding.

The aura of strangeness further expanded to encompass accounts of angelic apparitions descending upon the town of Point Pleasant, their ethereal presence casting an otherworldly glow upon the landscape. Alongside these celestial beings, orbs of light danced across the skies above the Ohio River, their movements defying the boundaries of the natural world and hinting at the presence of forces that eluded human comprehension.

But the strangeness did not stop at mere visual phenomena. Reports of power outages plunged the area into darkness, mirroring the uncertainty that had gripped the collective consciousness. People spoke of inexplicable time loss, recounting journeys that spanned hours but were shrouded in amnesia, as if time itself had been folded and manipulated by an unseen hand. The combined impact of these events created an environment where the boundaries of reality were blurred, where the mundane and the extraordinary converged in a mesmerizing dance.

In the wake of these perplexing events, a cast of otherworldly characters emerged, adding layers of intrigue and uncanniness to the events. Amidst this intricate tapestry of strangeness, one figure stood out with an air of profound enigma – Indrid Cold. Cold's appearances were not confined to mere chance encounters; rather, they unfolded within the context of inexplicable phenomena that defied rational explanation. Witnesses reported encountering Cold aboard mysterious spacecraft, a mode of transportation that transcended the boundaries of the ordinary. The method of communication attributed to Cold was equally unconventional – a telepathic exchange that bypassed the constraints of spoken language.

Equally unsettling were the appearances of individuals clad in black suits, a group that would later become infamously known as the Men In Black (MIB). These enigmatic figures exuded an air of anachronism, appearing out of place in both time and context. Their presence invoked a sense of unease, as if they were observers from a realm beyond our comprehension, intervening in the unfolding narrative writing letters under the guise of the International Bankers and warning witnesses to "stop talking about UFOs."

The wave of high strangeness led to Keel dubbing Point Pleasant as "a window area" to explain how the strange phenomena manifested there. When the window is closed, things appear to be more or less normal. But, when the window opens, all sorts of strange creatures from time and space come waltzing into the place.

There are many explanations offered for why Point Pleasant could be a so-called window area. These explanations range from geographical anomalies that possess unique energies to mysterious ley lines converging in the TNT area. I want to offer a theological explanation that could explain the metaphysics of Keel's "window area" concept.

Point Pleasant, West Virginia, stands as a unique and intriguing location—an embodiment of a liminal space, a concept referring to areas that exist in-between, defying clear categorization. This town is situated precisely at the convergence point of the Kanawha and Ohio Rivers, where the distinct boundaries between these two waterways blur and meld. Within liminal spaces, the familiar notions of identity and order undergo dissolution, giving rise to a sense of ambiguity, blurred lines, and disorder.

An illustrative example of this phenomena lies in the very confluence of the Kanawha and Ohio Rivers. At this juncture, the question arises: which river is dominant—Kanawha or Ohio? The merging of these waters defies easy differentiation, resulting in a breaking down of conventional identity and order.

Indigenous communities held a profound recognition of this liminality, stemming from their spiritually attuned worldviews. Evidencing this perspective, a ziggurat-shaped altar stone adorned with intricate carvings, known as the "water panther," remains a tangible relic on display at Tu-Endie-Wei State Park. In the tapestry of Native American mythology, the water panther emerged as an aquatic entity residing in the depths of lakes and rivers. These beings were intrinsically linked to elemental forces, their presence often heralding storms, misfortune, and even death. Consequently, the water panther demanded appeasement for safe passage across bodies of water.

The native belief in the water panther and the choice to etch a petroglyph of its image upon the altar stone not only echoes their recognition of Point Pleasant's liminal nature but also serves as a testament to their reverence for the spiritual dimensions inherent in these in-between spaces. The convergence of rivers, the melding of identities, and the deep-rooted symbolism of the water panther collectively contribute to Point Pleasant's status as a locus of transition and spiritual significance.

It is crucial to acknowledge that Point Pleasant's significance extends beyond its natural and geographical attributes. Historical records reveal that this very locale was also a site where the worship of pagan deities and principalities transpired. Such acts of worship have been understood, across various cultural and religious perspectives, to disrupt the sanctity of an area and introduce a defiling influence. The consequences of such actions have been observed to materialize through the manifestation of principalities within the geographical space, exerting their influence in diverse and often unsettling ways.

This isn't just the case in places like Point Pleasant, but also other window areas like Skinwalker Ranch in the Uinta Basin of Utah where rival native tribes waged war against one another.

This interplay between spiritual practices and the tangible world underscores a belief shared by many cultures: that the spiritual realm and the physical realm are intrinsically linked. The act of worshiping pagan gods in a specific locale is thought to leave a lingering imprint—an influence that can be felt and experienced. As the spiritual atmosphere becomes saturated with these intentions, it can attract and give rise to manifestations of principalities, spiritual entities often associated with specific domains or forces.

This idea is profoundly biblical. In the Bible, we see that spaces like this are places that manifest strange phenomena. As we've already seen beings like Azazel manifest themselves "outside of the camp of Israel" in the place of sin (Lev. 16). In other words, Israel was a set apart, sanctified geographical location because God was worshiped there in the temple. The places outside of that were domains of darkness and sin.

Commenting on this concept of sacred and profane space, Michael Heiser says:

> "I believe Azazel is best taken as a proper name of a demonic entity. In the Day of Atonement ritual, the goat for Yahweh—the goat that was sacrificed—purifies the people of Israel and the Tabernacle/Temple. Sins were "atoned for" and what had been ritually unclean was sanctified and made holy. But purification only described part of what atonement

meant. The point of the goat for Azazel was not that something was owed to the demonic realm, as though a ransom was being paid. The goat for Azazel banished the sins of the Israelites to the realm outside Israel. Why? Because the ground on which Yahweh had his dwelling was holy; the ground outside the parameters of the Israelite camp (or, nation, once the people were in the Land) had been consigned to fallen, demonic deities back at Babel. Sin could not be tolerated in the camp of Israel, for it was holy ground. Sins had to be "transported" to where evil belonged—the territory outside Israel under the control of gods set over the pagan nations. The high priest was not sacrificing to Azazel. Rather, Azazel was getting what belonged to him: the ugly sinfulness of the nation." [39]

What then is my perspective regarding the Mothman phenomenon?

In my view, Point Pleasant, West Virginia, can be understood as a liminal space that has undergone a form of defilement through the worship of principalities. When these spiritual entities are welcomed and granted authority over a specific geographic

---

[39] Michael Heiser, *The Day of Atonement in Leviticus 16: A Goat For Azazel* (Wellingham, WA; Dr. MSH website 2013), https://www.drmsh.com/day-atonement-leviticus-16-goat-azazel

region, their influence can manifest in diverse ways—ranging from UFO sightings and cryptid encounters to paranormal activities and other inexplicable anomalies.

A noteworthy element of consideration is the intriguing link between Mothman and the Thunderbird deity revered by the indigenous people of the region. Remarkably, during the initial sightings of Mothman, John Keel observed that the entity was referred to as "the bird" and even "the bird man." In my interpretation, I posit that Mothman could potentially have angelic origins and may even represent a principality that was venerated in the locality many centuries ago.

## Sirens and Mermaids

Amidst the diverse tapestry of cryptid sightings, tales of sirens and mermaids have consistently captured human imagination across cultures and eras. While often relegated to the realms of myth and folklore, modern-day Israel has emerged as a surprising hotspot for reported sightings of these aquatic mythic creatures, giving rise to intrigue and even official government attention.
In 2009, the Israeli city of Kiryat Yam became a focal point for an astonishing series of mermaid sightings. As the sun set over the

tranquil shoreline, dozens of locals reported encountering an enigmatic figure that defied conventional explanation. The creature, described as a fusion between a young girl and a fish, would appear offshore, captivating onlookers with her aquatic antics. Witnesses marveled at her apparent affinity for the beach, where she would perform mesmerizing tricks in the water, blurring the boundaries between the human and aquatic realms.

The frequency of these sightings prompted a curious response from the Israeli government. In an unprecedented move, authorities offered a staggering $1 million dollar reward for substantial evidence substantiating the existence of this mysterious marine entity. This government endorsement elevated the encounters from mere local anecdotes to a national topic of intrigue and investigation.

The gravity of the situation drew the attention of an NBC film crew, dispatched to Kiryat Yam to document and probe the reported sightings. Their mission involved capturing the essence of the beach both day and night, in hopes of uncovering definitive proof or clues that would shed light on the nature of these encounters. As the crew diligently observed, an event of significance occurred—an elusive human-like figure was spotted dipping into the water before mysteriously disappearing beneath the waves.

To assess the authenticity of this sighting, the captured footage was subjected to rigorous scrutiny. The Center for Coastal Ocean Research in Los Angeles, California, under the leadership of Director Michael Shacht, took on the task of analyzing the evidence. Shacht's assessment was both intriguing and enigmatic in itself. While he refrained from drawing definitive conclusions, he acknowledged that the possibility of an unknown entity occupying the waters remained a viable and valid option. The lingering uncertainty showcased the complexity of deciphering such phenomena, echoing the intricate nature of encounters that defy conventional classification. [40]

While the Kiryat Yam mermaid sightings captured substantial attention, they are by no means isolated occurrences. Across the globe, numerous locales have become associated with reported visits from these aquatic beings. In fact, communities have gone so far as to erect statues and monuments to commemorate these encounters, underscoring the enduring allure of the mythical realm that intersects with our own.

---
[40] Eti Dor, *NBC: Kiryat Yam Mermaid Might Be Real* (Tel Aviv, Israel; YNET News 2010), https://www.ynetnew.com/articles/0,7340,L-3883746,00.html

The widespread sightings of these mythic creatures across diverse cultures and geographic locations present a compelling challenge to the conventional tendency to dismiss such encounters as mere flights of fantasy. These consistent reports, spanning continents and centuries, underscore a perplexing truth: the allure of sirens and mermaids transcends cultural boundaries and endures through time, defying the tendency to simply write them off as mythical.

The very universality of these tales adds layers of complexity to this interpretation. From the enchanting lore of Greek mythology to the mystical narratives of Far Eastern cultures, the consistent presence of these aquatic beings in human stories reflects something profoundly universal that we must consider. The fact that individuals from distinct backgrounds, often separated by vast distances and centuries, have reported similar experiences adds weight to the legitimacy of these encounters.

So, how can we best interpret these encounters?
To the surprise of many, we actually see that these so-called mythical beings make their way into not just the literature of the Second Temple Period, but also the Bible itself.

The prophet Isaiah in Isaiah 13:21 spoke of the coming destruction of the Chaldeans and their cities. The interesting thing to note is how the translators of the Greek Septuagint (LXX) translated this passage. It says:

> "But wild animals will rest there, and the houses will be filled with noise, there sirens will rest, and there demons will dance. Donkey-centaurs will dwell there, and hedgehogs will build nests in their houses; It is coming quickly and will not delay."

Now, lest you think that the so-called mythical language is an oddity, it should be noted that even most english translations include the so-called mythical beings in translation of the text. For example, the King James Version (KJV), Aramaic Bible in Plain English (ABPE), English Revised Version (ERV), JPS Tanakh 1917 (JPS), New American Bible (NAB), New Revised Standard Version (NRSV), and Websters Bible Translation (WBT) all use the language of sirens, satryrs, goat demons, devils, and dragons in the texts. It's clear that this passage has not just natural creatures in view, but also supernatural creatures as well, even some that many would simply write off as mythical.

There is also a tradition in the Second Temple Period noted by scholars connecting the sirens to the "daughters of men" whom angels took in Genesis 6 and in 1 Enoch. Bautch comments on this stating:

> "It has long been noted that the Enochic corpus preserves a distinctive story concerning the origin of evil, an account that is known only partially from Genesis 6. Enochic works tell the story of angels who forsake their heavenly dwelling in order to mate with women. The union of angels and mortals results in bloodthirsty giants who scar the earth and abuse its inhabitants. The angels, or watchers as they are called, also contribute to humanity's decline by introducing all sorts of forbidden arts. Although these angels come to be imprisoned at the ends of the earth, their spirits continue to wreak havoc by inciting humans to commit idolatry (see 1 En. 19:1). Yet what of the women who associated with the watchers? As if an afterthought, 1 En. 19:2 briefly recounts the fate of these women as well. According to the Greek manuscript tradition, the wives of the angels who

transgressed are to become sirens, mythological creatures often associated with seduction." [41]

1 Enoch 19:1-3 sheds some light on this and seems to suggest that because the angels entered into sexual union with women, their spirits were able to assume many different forms, thus defiling mankind. The text reads:

> "And Uriel said to me: 'Here shall stand the angels who have connected themselves with women, and their spirits assuming many different forms are defiling mankind and shall lead them astray into sacrificing to demons as gods, [here shall they stand,] till the day of the great judgment in which they shall be judged till they are made an end of. And the women also of the angels who went astray shall become sirens.' And I, Enoch, alone saw the vision, the ends of all things: and no man shall see as I have seen."

In the tapestry of human understanding, sirens and mermaids, like cryptid phenomena at large, emerge as more than mere whims of imagination. Their persistent presence across cultures, histories, and religious texts challenges our conventional

---

[41] Kelley Coblentz Bautch, "What Becomes of the Angel's 'Wives'? A Text-Critical Study of 1 Enoch 19:2," *Journal of Biblical Literature* 125 (2006): 766.

paradigms and invites deeper contemplation. These encounters beckon us to journey beyond the familiar, embracing the enigmatic and embracing a broader understanding of reality—one that recognizes the intricate interplay between the mundane and the enchanted.

## Conclusion

The exploration of cryptid phenomena, from fairies to the Mothman and sirens, reveals a world that defies easy categorization. The conventional dichotomy between reality and myth becomes increasingly blurred as we delve into the intricacies of encounters that traverse cultural boundaries, epochs, and dimensions. In the context of Christian beliefs, these phenomena present a unique challenge—one that demands a nuanced perspective that goes beyond dismissing them as mere fabrications or demonized manifestations.

Cryptid phenomena, often relegated to the realm of myths and folklore, persist across cultures and time periods, challenging our understanding of reality. Fairies, with their connections to pagan deities and principality worship, embody a liminal space that straddles the boundaries of the seen and unseen. The Mothman of Point Pleasant, with its convergence of UFO sightings and inexplicable events, opens a window to the interplay between dimensions beyond our comprehension. The allure of sirens and mermaids spans continents and centuries, inviting us to consider the existence of a hidden realm that transcends our rational understanding.

As we confront the mysteries of these encounters, it becomes clear that a binary interpretation falls short. The mere dismissal of these phenomena as unreal or demonic overlooks the complex nature of their manifestations. Instead, an alternative perspective emerges—one that acknowledges the possibility of cryptids existing within a metaphysical reality that intersects with our own. Such an understanding allows for a deeper exploration of the relationship between the spiritual and physical realms, embracing the notion that the boundaries between them are porous and subject to interpenetration.

In this worldview, the enchanted and the mundane coexist, and the extraordinary seamlessly intertwines with the ordinary. The ancient belief in fairies as both ethereal and tangible entities finds echoes in the biblical concept of elemental spirits. The Mothman's presence becomes a manifestation of a principality, an angelic entity, imprinted on a defiled geographical space. The universal allure of sirens and mermaids bridges cultures and epochs, inviting us to contemplate a shared reality that defies our conventional understanding.

# 6

## Ghosts

## Introduction

As we conclude this book, it is imperative to delve into the intriguing realm of ghosts and haunting phenomena.

Similar to our discussions on UFOs, UAPs, and cryptids, the subject of ghosts and hauntings often faces skepticism within the Christian community. Many believers tend to diminish this kind of phenomena, dismissing it as mere inventions or again, demonic.

However, whenever we look at the Bible, it's clear that the biblical writers recognized the existence of ghosts – or the disembodied spirits of the deceased.

## The Ghost on the Water

In the Gospel of Matthew, we come across a curious account where the disciples of Jesus mistake him as a ghost. The texts says:

"22 And immediately he made the disciples get into the boat and go ahead of him to the other side, while he sent away the crowds. 23 And after he* sent away the crowds, he went up on the mountain by himself to pray. So when* evening came, he was there alone. 24 But the boat was already many stadia distant from the land, being beaten by the waves, because the wind was against it. 25 And in the fourth watch of the night he came to them, walking on the sea. 26 But the disciples, when they* saw him walking on the sea, were terrified, saying, "It is a ghost!" and they cried out in fear. 27"

The interesting thing about the word "ghost" is that in Greek it is φάντασμα or phantasma. The word, interestingly, doesn't mean demon but rather apparition, specter, or spirit. This is where our English word "phantasm" comes from.

Commenting on this, Michael Heiser writes:

> "Christians typically assume (and I hope you've heard the old bromide about what happens when we assume things) that ghosts are demons. This is simply not true, and it is

demonstrably untrue with respect to the biblical text (both testaments).

If you don't believe that, here's a quick proof before we actually get into the topic. In Matt. 14:26 the disciples react in fear when they see Jesus walking on the water. They scream out, "It's a ghost!" The Greek word for "ghost" here is phantasma. Any Greek-English dictionary (lexicon) or Strong's number search will reveal to you that this isn't the Greek word for "demon" in the New Testament. The disciples had a category for "disembodied spirit of a dead person" (a ghost). They didn't just think in demonic terms." [42]

## The Ghost of Samuel

Another passage that discusses ghosts or the disembodied spirits of deceased humans 1 Samuel 28:3-25. The text reads:

"3 (Now Samuel had died, and all Israel had mourned for him, and they had buried him in Ramah, his own city. And Saul had expelled the mediums and the soothsayers from

---

[42] Michael Heiser, *A Biblical View of Ghosts* (Wellingham, WA; Dr. MSH website 2008), https://www.drmsh.com/a-biblical-view-of-ghosts-part-1/#fnref-6512-1

the land.) 4 Then the Philistines assembled and came and encamped at Shunem, so Saul assembled all Israel, and they encamped at Gilboa. 5 When Saul saw the army of the Philistines, he was afraid and his heart trembled greatly. 6 And Saul inquired of Yahweh, but Yahweh did not answer him, not by dreams or by the Urim or by the prophets. 7 So Saul said to his servants, "Search for me ⌞a woman who is a medium⌟ so that I may go to her and inquire of her." His servants said to him, "Look there is a woman who is a medium in Endor." 8 So Saul disguised himself and put on other clothes, and he went ⌞with two of his men⌟. And they came to the woman by night and he said, "Please consult a spirit for me through ⌞the ritual pit⌟, and bring up for me the one whom I tell you." 9 But the woman said to him, "Look, you know what Saul did, how he exterminated the mediums and the soothsayers from the land! Why are you setting a trap for my life to kill me?" 10 Then Saul swore to her by Yahweh, "⌞As Yahweh lives⌟, ⌞you will not be punished⌟ for this thing." 11 So the woman asked, "Whom shall I bring up for you?" He said, "Bring up Samuel for me." 12 When the woman saw Samuel, she cried out with a loud voice, and the woman said to Saul, "Why did you deceive me? You are Saul!" 13 The king said to her, "Do not be afraid! What do you see?" And the woman said to Saul, "I see a god coming up from the ground!" 14 Then he said to her, "What is his appearance?" She said, "An old man is coming up, and ⌊he is wrapped in a robe⌋." Then Saul realized that it was Samuel, and he knelt with his face to the ground and bowed down. 15 Then Samuel said to Saul, "Why have you disturbed me by bringing me up?" And Saul said, "⌊I am in distress⌋! For the Philistines are about to make war against me, but God has turned away from me, and he does not answer me any more, not ⌊by the prophets⌋ or by the dreams. So I called to you to let me know what I should do." 16 Then Samuel said, "Why do you ask me, since Yahweh has turned away from you and has become your enemy? 17 Yahweh has done to you just as he spoke by my hand! Yahweh has torn the kingdom from your hand and has given it to your neighbor, to David. 18 Because you ⌊did not obey⌋ Yahweh and did not carry out the fierce anger of his ⌊wrath⌋ against Amalek, therefore Yahweh has done this thing to you today. 19 And Yahweh will also give Israel with you into the hands of the Philistines, and tomorrow you and your sons will be with me, and Yahweh will also give the army of Israel into the hand of the Philistines." 20 ⌊Then Saul immediately fell prostrate⌋ to the ground, and he was very afraid because of the words of Samuel; there was no more strength in him, for he had not eaten food all day and all night. 21 Then the woman came to Saul and realized that he was absolutely terrified, so she said to him, "Look, your female servant ⌊has obeyed you⌋, and I have ⌊risked my life⌋. I have listened to your words that you have spoken to me. 22 So then, you also please listen to the voice of your female servant, and let me set before you a morsel of bread, and you eat so that ⌊you will have strength⌋ in you when you go on your way." 23 But he refused and said, "I will not eat!" However, his servants urged him, and the woman also. So he listened ⌊to what they said⌋, and he got up from the ground and sat on the bed. 24 Now the woman had a fattened bull calf in the house, ⌊so she quickly slaughtered it⌋ and took flour, kneaded dough, and baked him some unleavened bread. 25 She brought it before Saul and his servants, and they ate. Then they got up and went away that very night."

In this passage, we gain insight into a pivotal event involving the Prophet Samuel following his demise. The entire nation of Israel mourns his passing and gives him a proper burial in Ramah. Meanwhile, the Philistine forces establish their camp at Shumen, prompting Saul, the king of Israel, to rally his people at Gilboa.

Confronted with the imposing Philistine army, Saul's heart is gripped with fear. Seeking guidance from Yahweh, he attempts to inquire of the divine, yet his entreaties go unanswered. Unbeknownst to Saul, the destiny of his kingdom has already been predetermined by Yahweh: it will be transferred from Saul's rule to that of David.

Desperate and driven by his quest for answers, Saul directs his servants to locate a necromancer. This necromancer is situated in Endor. Saul adopts a disguise and ventures to her abode under the cover of night. He implores her, "Please, perform a ritual to consult a spirit on my behalf." Notably, the term employed for "spirit" in Hebrew is "אוב" (ʾôḇ), which in this particular context signifies the "spirit of the deceased" or "ghost." It does not carry the connotation of a demon.

Saul explicitly requests the necromancer to conjure the spirit of Samuel. The narrative implies that the necromancer successfully conducts the required ritual to commune with the departed in the ritual pit. As a result, the spirit of Samuel emerges from the realm of the dead. The necromancer reacts with astonishment, exclaiming, "I see a divine being ascending from the earth." The term translated as "divine being" is "אֱלֹהִים" (ʾĕlō·hîm) in Hebrew, which can encompass meanings such as "spirit," "god," or "angel."

What's particularly intriguing is the absence of any textual indication that challenges the identity of the conjured entity as Samuel. Importantly, the term "demon" is conspicuously absent from the text. The scripture maintains the impression that Samuel's spirit is invoked from the realm of the deceased and imparts accurate information to King Saul, information that subsequently comes to fruition. This occurrence underscores the rationale behind Yahweh's prohibition of necromancy and spiritism within the context of the Law. The prohibition is not founded on the idea that these practices are ineffective, but rather on their effectiveness, as they hold the potential to invoke genuine spiritual interactions.

## Ghosts and Haunting Phenomena

Armed with this information, we can now adopt a biblically informed perspective when considering ghost and haunting phenomena. How should we approach and interpret such occurrences within the framework of our faith?

First and foremost, it's important to recognize that the Bible does acknowledge the existence of disembodied spirits or ghosts. As evidenced by passages like the encounter between Jesus and his disciples on the water, and the account of Saul consulting the spirit of Samuel, the biblical narrative doesn't outright dismiss the notion of spirits of the deceased being present in some form.

However, it's equally important to exercise discernment and caution. While the Bible acknowledges the existence of spirits, it also provides guidance against practices such as necromancy and spiritism. The prohibition against these practices stems from a concern not only for accurate representation but also for the potential dangers involved. Engaging in attempts to conjure or communicate with spirits, even if they are believed to be those of the deceased, can open doors to spiritual influences that may not align with God's intentions for us.

## Jesus and Ghosts of Old Testament Saints

This prompts a pertinent inquiry: If the Scriptures advise against engaging with spirits of the deceased, does that imply that Jesus engaged in necromancy when conversing with the spirits of Elijah and Moses during the Mount of Transfiguration (Matthew 17:1-9)?

To address this query directly, the answer is a resounding no.

The pivotal contrasts between the transfiguration event and necromancy are rooted in the manner of engagement and the underlying intention. Necromancy involves attempts to commune with deceased spirits via rituals and practices that directly oppose the precepts outlined in the Bible. These practices often stem from curiosity, the pursuit of knowledge, or even the quest for power.

However, the instance of the transfiguration sets itself apart in terms of initiation and purpose. Jesus' interaction with Elijah and Moses was not a result of human effort or ritualistic practices. Instead, it was initiated by the divine will of God for specific divine intentions. The transfiguration did not transgress God's guidelines but rather adhered to them, as it was orchestrated by God Himself.

This pivotal event served to unveil the profound nature of Christ's identity and mission, encapsulating both His divine nature and fulfillment of the Law and the Prophets. As such, it stands in stark contrast to necromancy, which seeks forbidden insights from the realm of the deceased through human manipulations.

## Ministers and Exorcism

However, what about the scenario where a minister finds themselves in the role of counseling an individual exhibiting signs of demonic manifestation? In this context, I have put forth the argument that a demon is the disembodied spirit of the deceased nephilim. The question that arises is whether such an interaction falls under the umbrella of necromancy.

It's crucial to discern the distinctions between these two scenarios. While there might be a surface similarity in the involvement of spiritual entities, the fundamental differences lie in the approach and purpose. Necromancy entails endeavors to communicate with departed spirits through rituals and practices that directly conflict with the teachings of the Bible. On the other hand, the minister's objective revolves around expelling the malevolent spirit through the authority of Christ. This act seeks to provide relief, healing, and deliverance from the spiritual affliction that the individual is facing.

The underlying intention becomes a significant factor in distinguishing between necromancy and the minister's role. Necromancers typically engage with the spirits of the deceased for personal gain, curiosity, or power. In stark contrast, the minister's motivation is to provide spiritual support, guidance, and liberation for the individual grappling with demonic manifestations. Their actions are grounded in the principles of Christianity, seeking to alleviate suffering and restore spiritual well-being. Additionally, the authority under which the minister operates plays a crucial role. The minister relies on the power and authority of Christ to confront and address spiritual entities. This aligns with the biblical precedent set by Jesus and his disciples, who cast out demons in his name. The intention is not to establish communication with the spirit but rather to invoke divine intervention for the person's benefit.

The distinction between a minister counseling someone manifesting a demonic spirit and necromancy lies in the underlying intention, the methodology employed, and the authority under which the actions are taken. The minister's role is fundamentally aligned with Christian principles of deliverance and healing, whereas necromancy involves forbidden practices rooted in self-interest and forbidden rituals.

# Conclusion

As we bring this exploration of ghosts and haunting phenomena to a close, we find ourselves navigating a realm that is both mysterious and fraught with misconceptions. Just as our discussions on UFOs, UAPs, and cryptids have unveiled the complexity of supernatural phenomena, the subject of ghosts and hauntings presents us with an opportunity to engage with biblical perspectives and wisdom.

One of the most intriguing aspects of this inquiry is the biblical recognition of the existence of ghosts – the disembodied spirits of the deceased. The encounter between Jesus and his disciples on the water, as recorded in the Gospel of Matthew, provides a significant example. The disciples' exclamation of "It's a ghost!" (Matthew 14:26) employs the Greek word "phantasma," which denotes an apparition, specter, or spirit, distinct from the term for "demon." This linguistic distinction, supported by biblical scholar Michael Heiser, underscores that the biblical narrative acknowledges a category for disembodied spirits.

Further illumination comes from the story of Saul consulting the spirit of Samuel, found in 1 Samuel 28:3-25. This account unveils the differentiation between necromancy and the engagement with spirits seen within Christian contexts. Saul's desperate attempt to communicate with the deceased Samuel through a necromancer in Endor highlights the forbidden nature of necromantic practices. However, this narrative doesn't negate the existence of interactions with the spirits of the deceased; rather, it underscores the biblical prohibition against specific means of seeking them. Informed by these insights, we navigate the nuanced landscape of ghosts and haunting phenomena with discernment and caution. While acknowledging that the Bible recognizes the existence of spirits, we heed its guidance against practices like necromancy and spiritism. These prohibitions are not based on inefficacy, but rather on the potential dangers and spiritual influences that such practices may invite. We recognize that engaging with departed spirits through rituals can open doors to spiritual forces that might not align with God's purposes.

Addressing the question of Jesus' interaction with the spirits of Elijah and Moses during the Transfiguration, we discern that this event diverges from necromantic practices. Initiated by God's divine will and purpose, this interaction serves to reveal the profound nature of Christ's identity and mission, standing in stark contrast to the forbidden manipulation of spirits.

Furthermore, we draw a clear distinction between the minister's role in counseling someone manifesting a demonic spirit and necromancy. The minister's actions, carried out under the authority of Christ, seek to provide healing, deliverance, and restoration for the afflicted individual. This stands in contrast to necromancy, which pursues forbidden insights through human manipulation and rituals. The intention and the methodology employed set these two scenarios apart, illustrating the alignment of the minister's role with Christian principles.

In conclusion, our journey through this chapter sheds light on the complexity of ghosts and haunting phenomena from a biblical perspective. By recognizing the existence of spirits while exercising discernment and obedience to biblical guidance, we navigate these mysteries with humility and wisdom, seeking to honor God and prioritize His purposes in all our explorations.

# Appendix A

# Re-enchanting The Unseen Realm

*The difference between the old Narnia and the new Narnia was like that. The new one was a deeper country: every rock and flower and blade of grass looked as if it meant more. I can't describe it any better than that: if ever you get there you will know what I mean.*

*It was the Unicorn who summed up what everyone was feeling. He stamped his right fore-hoof on the ground and neighed, and then he cried:*

*"I have come home at last! This is my real country! I belong here. This is the land I have been looking for all my life, though I never knew it till now. The reason why we loved the old Narnia is that it sometimes looked a little like this. Bree-hee-hee! Come further up, come further in!"- C.S. Lewis, The Last Battle*

**Introduction**

Are there horses in the unseen realm? What about gardens? What about cities with buildings?

A lot of work has been done to re-enchant our view of the inhabitants of the unseen realm. But, thus far, little has been done to re-enchant our view of the realm in which the inhabitants reside. I believe this work is also important, because it can give more weight and longing to live within the traditional cosmic imagery of Christendom.

The sad reality is that many Christians not only have a disenchanted view of the inhabitants of the unseen realm but the unseen realm itself.

When most think of the unseen realm, they think of a flat, shadowy realm or a heaven on the clouds where people are playing harps for eternity. But the reality is that it's livelier and more real than the realm we live in. It's filled with its own flora, fauna, and architecture. They're not just celestial beings who reside there, but archetypal beings as well.

**The Fauna of the Unseen Realm**

Though the modern conception of the unseen realm has been disenchanted by what I will call a dark enlightenment, the Bible presents a vision of the unseen realm that is enchanted. So enchanted, in fact, that there is even celestial fauna who reside there.

One of the passages comes from 2 Kings 6:15-17. It reads:

> "When the servant of the man of God got up and went out early the next morning, an army with horses and chariots had surrounded the city. "Oh no, my lord! What shall we do?" the servant asked.
>
> "Don't be afraid," the prophet answered. "Those who are with us are more than those who are with them."
>
> And Elisha prayed, "Open his eyes, Lord, so that he may see." Then the Lord opened the servant's eyes, and he

looked and saw the hills full of horses and chariots of fire all around Elisha."

In this passage, the city that Elisha is residing in is surrounded by an army with horses and chariots (Most likely the Arameans based off the previous chapter). Elisha's servant is frightened by the situation and says to Elisha "Oh no, my lord! What shall we do?" Elisha replies to him and tells him to not be afraid because he's aware of something that he is not.

What was he aware of? What was it that he was able to see that his servant couldn't?

It's apparent that Elisha and his servants saw two different realities before them. One saw in the spirit and the other saw in the flesh. Elisha saw the army of the Lord mustered upon horse and chariot burning with celestial fire, and it's not until the Lord opened the servants' eyes that he was able to see it too.

And so it is that our eyes are opened as well. At once we are met with the re-enchanting reality that the Lord has willed it to be that it wouldn't just be humanity who lives, moves, and has its being in the One who speaks the heavens and earth into existence, but even high creatures from a deep country we've not yet known.

This way of thinking about the unseen realm was common in the Ancient Near East.

When Marduk goes to war with the chaos dragon Tiamat in the Enuma Elish, he bears similitude to the warriors in the army of God in 2 Kings. He is depicted as a warrior with weapons, riding a celestial chariot with horses.

> "...He [Marduk] made the bow and weapon, brought forth the arrow and the quiver, Mounted the chariot, harnessed and yoked Four horses, destructive, overwhelming, Sharp of horn, he mounted the chariot He went forth, swift, irresistible, Proceeding like a hurricane." - Enuma Elish (Standard Akkadian Version), Tablet VII, Lines 121-127)

Are there really horses in the unseen realm? If there are, then does that mean that it's possible there are other kinds of fauna in the unseen realm? The Bible and the myths of the nations surrounding Israel seem to indicate that this is the case. There's certainly a symbolic nature to them in that they point to the realities of power and celestial status. However, that doesn't do away with the reality that the symbols really exist.

In the same way that bread and wine point to the realities of the broken body and shed blood of Christ, the fact that they point beyond themselves does not erase the reality of the symbol. They certainly participate in one another, but grace does not destroy nature. My personal thought is that there does seem to be fauna in the unseen realm and because I'm also a Christian Platonist, I don't see a reason for why there couldn't be other kinds of fauna in heaven as well. But I'll get to that more at the end.

**The Flora of the Unseen Realm**

The Bible also suggests to us that there is flora in the unseen realm. The flora that is suggested in being there is the Tree of Life.

In Genesis 3, God exiled the first man and woman from the Garden of Eden and the Tree of Life for their rebellion against Him. The question this raises is where did the Tree of Life go after that? Is it still out there somewhere, waiting to be rediscovered? Scientists and archeologists have been theorizing about their whereabouts for millennia. However, I believe that the Bible suggests that it was taken up into the unseen realm.

When we contemplate the unfolding of the biblical narrative, we see that the man's exile from the Edenic Tree is something that does not come to an end until the New Jerusalem comes down from out of heaven. In Revelation 21, John the Revelator gives us a mystical vision of the Age to Come when the City of God will come down from out of heaven to earth (Rev. 21:2). It's worthy of noting that it's then and only then that we see man having access once again to the Tree of Life. I believe this suggests that after man's exile from the Garden of God that it and the Tree were taken up into the City of God, and it was done so lest men reach out his hand and take of the Tree of Life and live forever (Gen. 3:22).

> "And he shewed me a pure river of water of life, clear as crystal, proceeding out of the throne of God and of the Lamb. In the midst of the street of it, and on either side of the river, was there the tree of life, which bare twelve manner of fruits, and yielded her fruit every month: and the leaves of the tree were for the healing of the nations. And there shall be no more curse: but the throne of God and of the Lamb

shall be in it; and his servants shall serve him: And they shall see his face; and his name shall be in their foreheads. And there shall be no night there; and they need no candle, neither light of the sun; for the Lord God giveth them light: and they shall reign for ever and ever." - Revelation 22:1-5

This thought is made much more explicit in the literature of the Second Temple Period which preceded the writing of Saint John's Apocalypse. It appears in several sources, but for purposes here I want to focus on 2 Enoch. In 2 Enoch 8:1-5, the writer states that the Tree of Life and Garden of Eden was located in the Third Heaven. He writes:

"About the taking of Enoch to the 3$^{rd}$ heaven.

And those men took me from there, and they brought me up to the third heaven, and set me down |there|. Then I looked downward, and I saw Paradise. And that place is inconceivably pleasant.

And I saw the trees in full flower. And their fruits were ripe and pleasant-smelling, with every food in yield and giving off profusely a pleasant fragrance.

And in the midst (of them was) the tree of life, at that place where the LORD takes a rest when he goes into paradise. And that tree is indescribable for pleasantness and fine fragrance, and more beautiful than any (other) created thing that exists." - 2 Enoch 8:1-5

The thought of flora existing in the unseen realm is not something foreign to the world picture of biblical writers and those writing in the Second Temple Period. It's also not foreign to the world picture of the rest of the Ancient Near East.

Again, in the Enuma Elish, Marduk was said to stretch out the heavens and found the earth. After he created them, he covered the dry land by unleashing the waters upon them, making them fruitful.

"He (Marduk) created dust, and he created the clouds. He spread out the heavens and he founded the earth below. He unleashed the waters and made them bear fruit. He established the Tigris and the Euphrates. The stars of heaven he fixed in their place. He measured out the year and marked the divisions. He set up the stations of Nibiru to determine their astral significance. After he had founded the earth and created the heavens, he created the estate of the great gods. The great gods entered the estate of the great gods. In the center of the estate of the great gods, he made the Garden of the Sun." - Enuma Elish, Tablet VI, Lines 1-15

Now, we must acknowledge that these sources referred to here are not Scripture. The Enochian literature is not inspired by God. Obviously the Babylonian Enuma Elish isn't either. However, the point that I'm making is that the thought of flora present in the unseen realm is not foreign to the world picture of the Ancient Near East, including the world picture of Israel.

**The Architecture of the Unseen Realm**

The Bible also is very clear that there is architecture in heaven. There, within its sacred, re-enchanting pages we see that God not only has a City, but even an armory within its celestial walls.

> "The LORD has opened his armory and brought out the weapons of his wrath, for the Lord GOD of hosts has a work to do in the land of the Chaldeans." - Jeremiah 50:25

It isn't much of a leap to see that this is where the celestial chariots and weaponry of the army of heaven that was seen earlier would be located. This may sound mythical, but we must remember that Christianity does not come to abolish myth. Christianity fulfills the great myths as the True Myth, as Tolkien said. Christians need not fear mythic elements in their world picture Rather, they need to fear the demythologized world picture that has been imposed upon them by the dark enchanted world picture of modernity.

The City of God is described in John the Revelator's apocalypse in this way:

> "Then came one of the seven angels who had the seven bowls full of the seven last plagues and spoke to me, saying, "Come, I will show you the Bride, the wife of the Lamb." And he carried me away in the Spirit to a great, high mountain, and showed me the holy city Jerusalem coming down out of heaven from God, having the glory of God, its radiance like a most rare jewel, like a jasper, clear as crystal. It had a great, high wall, with twelve gates, and at the gates twelve angels, and on the gates the names of the twelve tribes of the sons of Israel were inscribed— on the east three gates, on the north three gates, on the south three gates, and on the west three gates. And the wall of the city had twelve foundations,

and on them were the twelve names of the twelve apostles of the Lamb.

And the one who spoke with me had a measuring rod of gold to measure the city and its gates and walls. The city lies foursquare, its length the same as its width. And he measured the city with his rod, 12,000 stadia. Its length and width and height are equal. He also measured its wall, 144 cubits by human measurement, which is also an angel's measurement. The wall was built of jasper, while the city was pure gold, like clear glass. The foundations of the wall of the city were adorned with every kind of jewel. The first was jasper, the second sapphire, the third agate, the fourth emerald, the fifth onyx, the sixth carnelian, the seventh chrysolite, the eighth beryl, the ninth topaz, the tenth chrysoprase, the eleventh jacinth, the twelfth amethyst. And the twelve gates were twelve pearls, each of the gates made of a single pearl, and the street of the city was pure gold, like transparent glass.

And I saw no temple in the city, for its temple is the Lord God the Almighty and the Lamb. And the city has no need of sun or moon to shine on it, for the glory of God gives it light, and

> its lamp is the Lamb. By its light will the nations walk, and the kings of the earth will bring their glory into it, and its gates will never be shut by day—and there will be no night there. They will bring into it the glory and the honor of the nations. But nothing unclean will ever enter it, nor anyone who does what is detestable or false, but only those who are written in the Lamb's book of life." - Revelation 21:9-27

Again, there's obvious symbolism in the passage. However, we must keep in mind once more that this doesn't do away with the reality that is being pointed at. The City of God — which is the perfect, archetypal City where the Council of God resides will one day come back down to earth. Heaven and earth be re-joined once more in a cosmic, holy wedlock and there will be no death that will be able to part the two henceforth.

This thought of there being architecture in the unseen realm is also present, once again, in the literature of the Second Temple Period. The writer of 1 Enoch describes the City of God in a very similar way, stating:

> "And the vision was shown to me thus: Behold, in the vision clouds invited me and a mist summoned me, and the course

of the stars and the lightnings sped and hastened me, and the winds in the vision caused me to fly and lifted me upward, and bore me into heaven. And I went in till I drew nigh to a wall which is built of crystals and surrounded by tongues of fire: and it began to affright me. And I went into the tongues of fire and drew nigh to a large house which was built of crystals: and the walls of the house were like a tesselated floor (made) of crystals, and its groundwork was of crystal. Its ceiling was like the path of the stars and the lightnings, and between them were fiery cherubim, and their heaven was (clear as) water. A flaming fire surrounded the walls, and its portals blazed with fire. And I entered into that house, and it was hot as fire and cold as ice: there were no delights of life therein: fear covered me, and trembling got hold upon me. And as I quaked and trembled, I fell upon my face. And I beheld a vision, And lo! there was a second house, greater than the former, and the entire portal stood open before me, and it was built of flames of fire. And in every respect it so excelled in splendour and magnificence and extent that I cannot describe to you its splendour and its extent. And its floor was of fire, and above it were lightnings and the path of the stars, and its ceiling also was flaming fire. And I looked and saw therein a lofty throne: its appearance was as crystal, and the wheels thereof as the shining sun, and there was the vision of cherubim. And from underneath the throne came streams of flaming fire so that I could not look thereon. And the Great Glory sat thereon, and His raiment shone more brightly than the sun and was whiter than any snow. None of the angels could enter and could behold His face by reason of the magnificence and glory and no flesh could behold Him. The flaming fire was round about Him, and a great fire stood before Him, and none around could draw nigh Him: ten thousand times ten thousand (stood) before Him, yet He needed no counselor. And the most holy ones who were nigh to Him did not leave by night nor depart from Him. And until then I had been prostrate on my face, trembling: and the Lord called me with His own mouth, and said to me: ' Come hither, Enoch, and hear my word.' And one of the holy ones came to me and waked me, and He made me rise up and approach the door: and I bowed my face downwards." - 1 Enoch 14:8-25

## Conclusion

I realize that what I'm putting forth here may sound foreign to modern ears. However, the reality is this is very ingrained in the Christian Tradition. By living within a re-enchanted cosmic imagery and world picture, we're far less likely to fall under the dark enchantment of modernity and its cosmic imagery. There is nothing that I am proposing here that hasn't been said since before the wheel of time turned to our current darkened age. Saint Augustine has said it this way:

> "For this [heavenly] Jerusalem is the mother of us all, and it is in heaven that the ideals exist, of which these things here below are but the copies." — Saint Augustine, City of God (Book XI, Chapter 26)

In other words, everything that exists here in the earth below are simply imperfect copies that participate in their perfect ideal that is present in the heavenly unseen realm. This is a profound notion. It is profound because it means in that deep heavenly country, the trees and gardens are greener, the animals are livelier, and the architecture is sublime. When the wheel of time turns for the final time, the heavenly City of God will come back to earth.

I imagine that there's an entire world unseen and untouched by man that we will one day explore and enjoy to the glorious praise of God's name. I don't believe we can currently fathom the perfections and varieties of celestial beings, life, and cities that await us. There will be rivers flowing from the Holy City that will be wetter, mountains that will be more glorious than those of Appalachia, and light that will kiss our skin in a way that the sun's rays never have. There are regions waiting for the sons of God to one day explore them. But, before that world comes, we must be planted like seed in the ground first, awaiting our eternal spring.

I believe that becoming aware of our own cosmic imagery and world picture matters. Not only does it produce meaning, weight, beauty, and longing, but it's also a much better alternative than the nihilism and rootlessness of modernity. The reality is that not only is our modern view of heaven inconsistent with the cosmic imagery that has come from the Bible and the world that it was born in (The Ancient Near East), but it also produces what we know won't be in heaven — tears of boredom. We are called to rule over the image below because we're images of our Father who rules over that which is above, and one day we'll rule over it with Him.

So, come further up, and further in!

# Appendix B

# Yahweh & The Gods of the Nations

**Introduction**

In the last chapter, we talked about the Unseen Realm and what the Bible tells us about it. In this chapter, we're going to begin to look deeper into the inhabitants of that realm.

In the opening pages of the Bible, we discover that the universe which we inhabit was created by an all-powerful, all-knowing, and all-present Elohim. We learn that He is such a powerful God that He simply speaks and worlds come into existence (Gen. 1:3). He exists outside of time and space, thus His knowledge is not bound by it. Indeed, it was Him who hung the sun, moon, and stars in the heavens to keep time (Gen. 1:14-19). We also learn that though He is transcendent and sits enthroned above the heavens in the Empyrean, He is also present in creation, hovering over the waters (Gen. 1:1-2).

It is in Him that all things live, move, and have their being (Acts 17:28). In Him, all things were created, both in heaven and on earth, visible and invisible, whether thrones or dominions or rulers or authorities. All things were created through Him and for Him (Col. 1:16). As the story progresses, we learn that this Elohim's name is Yahweh (Ex. 6:3) and that there are no gods like Him.

Now, when you read the source material of the Ancient Near East, you realize that the gods of the nations are depicted quite differently than Yahweh. In the Bible, Yahweh is depicted as a deity who has complete power over His creation, and yet who is also imminent and present within it. This isn't the case with the gods of the nations. The gods of the nations are limited, created beings that are bound to the same limitations and imperfections as humans.

For example, in the Ugaritic poem *Baal and Anath*, Baal is depicted as being defeated by the god Mot and descending to the underworld. This suggests that Baal is subject to fate and is not all-powerful like Yahweh. Additionally, in the same poem, Baal's sister Anat expresses concern for his safety and is shown to be able to take action to help him, which further suggests that he is not completely all-powerful.

In the Babylonian creation myth *Enuma Elish*, Marduk is shown as having to negotiate with the other gods and convince them to give him their powers so that he can defeat the chaos dragon Tiamat. Again, like with Baal, this suggests that Marduk is not all-powerful and must rely on the help of others. Additionally, in some versions of the myth, Marduk is shown as having to use trickery to defeat Tiamat, which suggests that not only is Marduk not omnipotent, but that Tiamat is not omniscient.

In ancient Egyptian texts, Thoth is frequently referred to as the god of writing, knowledge, and wisdom, but he is not depicted as all-knowing or all-powerful. For example, in the *Coffin Texts* which are a collection of funerary spells from the Middle Kingdom period, Thoth is shown as having to rely on other gods to help him defeat his enemies:

> "O Thoth, thou hast come to bring the Ogdoad and put an end to the slaughter. But take care lest thy heart be not led away by it, lest the Slaughterer lay hold of thee. For thou art not mighty to deal with it alone." - Coffin Text, Spell 148

This example suggests that Thoth, like the other gods, is not completely all-powerful and must rely on the help of others.

In his work *The Gods of the Nations: A Study in Ancient Near Eastern National Theology*, Dr. Daniel Block notes that in ancient near eastern theology, there was an understood spectrum with divinities ranging from household gods to cosmic gods whose influence varied greatly. Block says:

> "According to the religious conceptions of all ancient Near Easterners, the affairs of the world in general and people in particular were subject to the wills and the actions of the gods. The sphere of influence of these divinites varied greatly, ranging from the limited authority of household deities, as, for example, in the case of the teraphim, to the universal sovereignty exercised by the cosmic gods, most notably the heads of pantheons, such as Enlil in Sumer and Akkad, El at Ugarit, and Zeus at Greece. Between these two extremes a host of intermediate gods was recognized. One group, defined essentially in functional terms, included divinities such as the storm god (Baal-Hadad) and the goddess of war (Anath). The authority of others, such as the god of the sea (Yamm at Ugarit) or the gods of the

mountains, was subject to geographical qualification." - Daniel Block, The Gods of the Nations, Pages 18-19

This is interesting in light of the source material we've already considered because it reveals that all of the gods of the ancient near east and even the greco-roman world were limited in some sense. In the myths and legends of the nations, the gods were depicted as having a sphere of influence, but not complete influence. Household gods were limited to exerting influence over a household. Gods that were higher in the hierarchy of being were limited to exerting influence over the elements, certain crafts as patron gods, or geographical areas like temples. Even cosmic gods who served as the head of the council of the gods were limited in some sense as well.

For example, In the Ugaritic Baal Cycle, El was depicted as a cosmic king who ages and declines in power and eventually gives way to Baal becoming the head of the council of gods. In the Babylonian Enuma Elish Enlil struggles for power against the gods and is eventually usurped by Marduk who becomes the head of the council of the gods. In Hesiod's *The Shield of Heracles* and in Sophocles' *The Woman of Trachis* Zeus is depicted as susceptible to the seductions of mortal women and subject to the whims of fate.

**The Death of the Gods**

This is some of what sets apart Yahweh from the gods of the nations. He is omnipotent, omniscient, and omnipresent, and the gods of the ancient world are not. Make no mistake, they're real. When Pythia, the Oracle of Delphi, became possessed in the manic bay at the Temple in Delphi, she was really possessed by the spirit of Apollo. But the gods of the nations aren't Yahweh and aren't like Yahweh.

The story of the Bible ultimately goes on to tell us why they're not. Ultimately, they're a part of the angelic hierarchy that Dionysius the Areopagite teaches us about. They're the thrones, dominions, powers, and authorities created by Yahweh who served in His council that was supposed to serve as ministering spirits to the people by leading them to the knowledge of the glory of God (Heb. 1:14). They're the sons of God who became the gods of the nations by committing treason against Yahweh the Most High (Gen. 11; Deut. 32:8).

It is for this reason that Yahweh steps into His divine council in Psalm 82 and declares that though they're gods, they'll die like men and that He would arise and re-inherit the nations that they caused to wander about in the darkness. The gods are inferior to Him for He alone dwells in unapproachable light.

In his City of God, Saint Augustine said it this way:

> "These gods of the nations, then, who are regarded as ruling over the regions of the earth and the courses of the stars, are believed to be superior to man in power and honour, but are believed to be inferior to the One True God in dignity." - Saint Augustine, The City of God, Book 11, Chapter 1

**Now We're The Sons of God**

This work of re-inheriting the nations is exactly what Yahweh accomplished in the death, burial, resurrection, and ascension of His eternally begotten Son - Jesus Christ. The head of the divine council reconciled people from every tribe tongue and nation to

Himself and disarmed the rulers, principalities, and powers of the darkness in heavenly realms.

Saint Paul says it this way:

> "And you, who were dead in your trespasses and the uncircumcision of your flesh, God made alive together with him, having forgiven us all our trespasses, by canceling the record of debt that stood against us with its legal demands. This he set aside, nailing it to the cross. He disarmed the rulers and authorities and put them to open shame, by triumphing over them in him." - Colossians 2:13-15

We must keep in mind that Paul isn't simply talking about earthly rulers and authorities, but also spiritual rulers and authorities. There is an "on earth as it is in heaven" dynamic at play. This is the same language used by Saint Paul elsewhere in Ephesians 6 to describe the cosmic powers over this present darkness who are the spiritual forces of evil in the heavenly places (Compare Col. 2:13-15 and Eph. 6:12).

Christ has disarmed these powers in His cosmic work. Their hold on the nations has been forever broken in a way that it wasn't previously. Christ is victorious in a way that the old gods were not. Rather than being enthroned in the midst of the council through usurpation like Marduk or through declining power and the need for succession like Baal, Jesus is enthroned as the One who rides the clouds because He came to honor His father by being obedient to His will (John 17:5; Phil. 2:8; Heb. 5:8).

This event has allowed for what Tolkien called "The True Myth" to spread to the four corners of the earth, and for those who are united to the God who created them to be re-enchanted. The old sons of God have been cast out from the council of God, and now because they have been thrown down we have the opportunity to become sons of God through adoption into the family of God (Eph. 3:20). We now get the opportunity to be reunited to God's divine council just as Adam was in the Garden of God. And, it is for this reason that we see elders standing in the midst of the council of God in Saint John's Revelation when previously we only saw angelic beings.

> "And round about the throne were four and twenty seats: and upon the seats, I saw four and twenty elders sitting, clothed

> in white raiment; and they had on their heads crowns of gold." - Revelation 4:4

This is what we were created for. To rule and reign with God as sons of God like the gods of the nations were supposed to. We were lifted up from the dust of the ground to be imagers of God and to share in His dominion over what we rose from. And because of the work of Christ, we are being restored to this and will finally be restored to this when the City of God comes down out of heaven to be rejoined with earth. We are moving from glory to glory.

Printed by Amazon Italia Logistica S.r.l.
Torrazza Piemonte (TO), Italy

54553736R00107